Two Bachelors Discover the Secrets of
America's Greatest Marriages

Project
everlasting

MATHEW BOGGS AND JASON MILLER

A FIRESIDE BOOK
PUBLISHED BY SIMON & SCHUSTER
NEW YORK   LONDON   TORONTO   SYDNEY

Fireside
A Division of Simon & Schuster, Inc.
1230 Avenue of the Americas
New York, NY 10020

For information about special discounts for bulk purchases,
please contact Simon & Schuster Special Sales at
1-800-456-6798 or business@simonandschuster.com.

Designed by Jan Pisciotta

Manufactured in the United States of America

10   9   8   7   6   5   4   3   2   1

Library of Congress Cataloging-in-Publication Data

Boggs, Mathew.
    Project everlasting / by Mathew Boggs & Jason Miller.
        p.   cm.
    "A Fireside Book."
    1. Marriage.   2. Marriage—Case studies.   3. Courtship—Case
    studies.   I. Title.
HQ734.B6664   2007
306.85—dc22   2007001229

ISBN-13: 978-1-4165-4325-1
ISBN-10:   1-4165-4325-2

Dedicated to

Jack and Dorothy Manin,

married sixty-three years

Contents

Prologue

A charming couple in their early sixties sits side by side in chairs. Expressions polite but skeptical, they watch as two young guys prepare for the interview, one loading a fresh tape into his video camera, the other scanning through a lengthy list of questions in his notebook.

The wife gets up to offer their guests more coffee. The husband clears his throat. "So you want to know all about our marriage, do you?" he asks the visitors.

"Yes, sir. We do."

"Remind me again, you're marriage therapists?"

"Not exactly."

"Doing academic research?"

"No, sir."

"And you're writing a book . . ."

"Yes, sir."

"And you are married, aren't you?"

"No, sir, we hope to be someday, but these days, it seems like a risky venture."

"Hmmm . . . bachelors writing a marriage manual . . ."

"Yes, sir. And we're seeking advice from the experts."

Then the camera begins to roll . . .

Introduction

NOW *THAT'S* THE MARRIAGE I WANT!

— by Mat

My favorite movie growing up was Walt Disney's animated *Robin Hood*—I watched it about a zillion times. Why? Because only a hero as cunning and courageous and charming as Robin Hood could get a girl like Maid Marian.

Oh, Maid Marian. (I understand that she's a cartoon fox, but she's a smokin' cartoon fox.) She had a sweet, contagious laugh that made me melt. She played badminton (extra points for being athletic). My heart literally pounded when Robin Hood and Maid Marian took a midnight stroll behind a waterfall.

Robin may have had to win his archery competition against the sheriff to get a kiss, but love conquers all, right? At age ten, that's what I believed. Never for a moment did I doubt the existence of everlasting love or my ability to obtain it. Happily ever after—isn't that what everyone wants?

Cut to several years later. I was studying for my ninth-grade biology test when my mom's voice broke the silence. Family meeting, she announced. This meant one of two things: Someone had either done something really right or really wrong. My family is full of overachievers, so I was more accustomed to celebrations than bad news. The second I stepped into the living room, however, I knew we wouldn't be celebrating anytime soon.

My sister sat on one end of our couch, my parents on the other. Mom was crying. She wiped away her tears and looked at me with eyes that said, *No matter what, you'll be okay.* This only worried me more. Dad, the consummate clown and entertainer, was expressionless. My parents did not touch.

My mom said, "Your dad and I have something to tell you— we're getting a divorce."

My stomach went into zero gravity and my sister burst into tears. Several of my friends had gone through this, but their parents were completely different from mine. Their parents screamed and threw plates at one another. Divorce was a godsend to those friends, not a tragedy. My parents' split came with no warning as far as I was concerned. They'd been married twenty-seven years and seemed like the happiest couple in the world. "I love you," they'd tell each other, and I believed them.

My mother's words obliterated everything I believed about love. Both my parents had betrayed me.

Lying in bed that night, my thoughts swirled so violently I became dizzy. Memories of my parents kissing and hugging, laughing, telling me over and over again, "We are soul mates, Mat," seemed like a mirage. *How could this happen? How could they have lied to me?*

Like most children of divorce, I was soon forced to make a decision: live out of a suitcase or pick a parent. I chose the suitcase. Every other weekend brought the bitter reminder that my home had been ripped in half. I felt turned inside out. Nothing felt familiar. The future loomed like a thick fog. *What will happen to Christmas? Birthdays? Thanksgiving?*

The divorce consumed all of our lives. I hated my mom for leaving my dad and I let her know it. I hated my dad for not being able to make my mom happy and I let him know it. I wanted my parents to love each other again. I wanted my family back, but it was hopeless. Apparently a commitment to forever lasted only until you changed your mind.

Thirteen years later, I was finishing my master's degree in education. My girlfriend and I were going through a nasty breakup. This relationship had lasted almost a year, a record for me.

My mom called from Portland to let me know my grandfather had been diagnosed with terminal cancer. Grandpa Jack dying? It didn't seem possible. I'd loved that warm, generous man for as long as I could remember and somehow thought he'd be around forever.

"You'll be home soon," my mom said. "You need to spend some time with your grandparents, maybe arrange a date each week."

Hang out with the grandparents? Of course I would. It's just that my schedule . . . I've got a lot on my plate . . . Don't get me wrong. When I was little, I idolized Grandma Dorothy and Grandpa Jack. They lived in a world of Mickey Mouse pancakes, a garden with candy hidden in it, and endless supplies of home-made cookies. They told funny stories about the olden days and thought everything I said was clever and important. They treated me like a little prince, and there was no place better than Gram and Gramps's house to find a warm hug.

My grandparents had always seemed old to me, but in a good, twinkly kind of way. In recent years, however, I'd found myself restlessly tapping my foot as I waited for them to put on their coats. They moved slowly, and I was in a perpetual hurry. I found it hard to sit through a two-hour lunch while Grandpa chewed each mouthful forty-four times and talked about the childhood friend who just died, especially when I had a ten-page term paper due.

Grandpa and Grandma were quaint and sweet and I loved them, but somewhere along the way my adoration had turned to tolerance. They listened politely but blankly when I talked about buying a laptop. And I could hardly share my girlfriend troubles with Gram and Gramps. They were the product of a bygone era. It had been, what, nearly sixty years since they had fallen in love? They probably didn't even remember what it felt like. In their day, people married for life because they didn't have a choice. Husbands worked, wives stayed home, and divorce was taboo. Even if a wife wanted out, how could she support herself? Now that couples can split up, they do—in droves. For my grandparents' generation, it seemed to me that marriage had become a habit that just took too much effort to break. But despite the fact that we lived on two different planets, they were still my grandparents.

"Of course, I'll spend time with them," I assured my mom. "Looking forward to it."

Guilt and obligation can sap the joy out of any activity, but I did come up with what sounded like a decent plan. Each Thursday morning I'd roll up to their house for the day's excursion. Grandma would spend the prior week combing the newspaper for that week's latest and greatest lunch spot. With newspaper clippings in hand, we'd hit the road, Grandma riding shotgun and Gramps sitting in the back, with the calm of someone who has made his peace with life. We would drive two or three hours in search of special treats in out-of-the-way spots, like Mike's pumpkin milk shakes, Dooger's clam chowder, and Serendipity's rich chocolate brownie cake.

To my great surprise, I had a blast on these visits. The long drives provided ample opportunity to learn things I never knew about my grandparents. Conversations that would have normally been cut off by typical interruptions—a phone call, an appointment, the football game—continued on into uncharted territory. I heard the story of their first date, how Grandma's dress popped open while they were dancing and how my brave grandfather nearly lost his fingers to hopping heels as he scurried around the dance floor on hands and knees, collecting all of the buttons. Gramps told me how nervous he felt meeting Grandma's parents for the first time—seeing their cat licking its back and hoping for a conversation starter, he commented, "I wish I could do that." But when her parents looked down, the cat was licking its crotch!

One crisp fall day, we went antiquing, Gram's favorite pastime. Dusty old furnishings and knickknacks hold zero interest for me, and it was our ninth trinket shop stop that day. I wearily pulled Gramps's Buick over and helped them out of the car. My grandparents went ahead as I locked up. I watched their slow, uneven shuffle toward the store. This was a standard sight by then, but something in that day, something in that moment, gave me pause. I noticed how their frail fingers were intertwined.

"Funny," I thought, "all these years, and they're still holding hands."

Suddenly, I stood there almost paralyzed, my eyes fixated on their hands. I know this sounds strange but the energy between them became visible. Like a movie effect, everything around them dissolved. I could see the energy of their love swirling and encircling them. It took me a second, but I got it. I remembered the longing for my true love, my Maid Marian, and my belief that our love would last forever. I hadn't had that feeling in years. I had long since abandoned the idea of everlasting love as a stupid fairy tale cartoon. Yet here it was in the flesh.

My chest began to tingle. In that moment, the couple before me became more than just my grandparents. I saw them as partners who had journeyed through a lifetime of challenge and struggle. Now at the end of their journey together, they were still crazy about each other. All these years . . . how had I not seen it? Grandpa beaming at Grandma, telling everyone in earshot, "Just look at her. Isn't she beautiful?" Grandma still laughing at jokes I'd heard Grandpa tell countless times. How his face lit up whenever she walked into a room! Through tear-filled eyes, I stared at the blurry image before me. How simple they made it seem! But to me it represented what I wanted most in the world. More than anything, I wanted to find the love they were living. My grandparents had been married sixty-three years, but it was not convention or habit that kept them together. Jack and Dorothy Manin were two people very much in love.

"Now, *that's* the marriage I want," I whispered to myself.

My grandfather passed away just a few months after that. Later, when she could talk about it, my grandma said it felt as if half of her had died with him.

After his death, I felt an overwhelming need to preserve the precious something that the two of them had shared. Hundreds of questions ran through my head: Were my grandparents an anomaly, the lone couple that just happened to remain happily married through the decades? Or could it be that other couples married forty, fifty, or sixty years were still in love, too? If so, how did they create and maintain that powerful connection? Way back when, how did they know they'd found "the One"? Didn't they worry about falling out of love one day? Or becoming bored? Was their longevity the result of dumb luck? Or could it be they had built something in their relationship that eluded most of the recent generations? If so, I wanted to know what that something was. I wanted to be madly in love with my wife on our golden anniversary. I wanted to look at her timeworn face and still see the most beautiful woman in the world. Thanks to my grandparents, I once more believed in lifelong love and I decided I would willingly crisscross the nation in search of what I'd started calling "Marriage Masters"—couples who'd been happily married for forty years or more, human treasure chests full of incredible wisdom, just waiting for someone to ask: *What is the secret to everlasting love?*

The adventure was about to begin.

DIFFERENT STROKES FOR DIFFERENT BLOKES

— by Jason

When my best friend Mat called and asked if I was game for a cross-country adventure, I said yes before asking the nature of the project. *The Mat and Jason Show* had always been a success. Our antismoking poster received the blue ribbon in third grade. Mat as Santa and Jason as Santa's most trusted pirate brought the house down in sixth grade. Our stimulate-all-the-senses, allegorical board game based on Dante's *Inferno* (complete with clay volcanoes, bloodlike magma, and soft yet sinister self-empowerment audio chanting in the background) got us an easy A in high school humanities. Somehow, despite my penchant for procrastination and Mat's tomfoolery, we did really well as project partners. And we always had a lot of fun in the process.

But then he told me about this quest for geriatric true love he wanted to do and I couldn't help it, I burst out laughing. Old people seemed pretty out of touch to me, so I couldn't imagine their marital advice being particularly germane. Besides, unlike Mat, I cherished bachelorhood. Settle down? Uh-uh, no thanks, I'll stick to what I know.

Really, what could these *Ozzie and Harriet*, Great Depression types have to say that applied to relationships of the twenty-first century? I began barraging Mat with questions regarding relevance: What do these old folks know about soccer moms or metrosexuality? How will their wisdom work for MySpace wife-browsing? I pointed out that what with online dating, e-cards, anytime minutes, and text messages, we inhabited an on-demand world that moved at the speed of "click," processing more information in twenty-four hours than the generation of a century ago processed in an entire year. How could older folks relate to all that?

And I had no immediate interest in the subject of matrimony. Flight patterns of Nigerian nightingales would have been just as personally meaningful a subject to research. The last time I'd had a real relationship was during college, and I'd wounded that woman's heart sufficiently to know that I wasn't ready to be serious again. Although my parents were happily married, plenty of other people around me were not, and I'm not sure I bought the whole concept of lifelong love.

Truthfully, marriage scared me.

I don't think I'm alone in that fear; wedlock seems to be an iffy endeavor to a lot of folks in my generation, and increasingly so. Studies show marriage rates declining every year: For the first time in U.S. history, married people are now in the minority. Americans are delaying marriage until they're older. The majority of today's couples now live together before marriage in order to scope things out and "make sure this is really the person I want to be with for the rest of my life"—something that was virtually unheard-of fifty years ago. Despite the statistics, I'd watched Mat's search for a woman so right for him that divorce wouldn't be an option. I'd found myself doing the same. I'd listened to friends talk about the need to become economically set before even thinking about marriage, insisting that this way money management conflicts, the ostensible root cause "for all of those divorces out there," would be altogether avoided. I'd nodded my head in agreement because I'd made the same excuse. I'd even read of a groom who replaced the "for as long as we both shall live," or the more traditional version, "till death do us part," with "until our time together is over." I'm no sociologist, but it was clear to me that all this practicality meant we were spooked.

Whether we've grown up with firsthand experience of divorce or simply witnessed our friends' struggles to cope with it in their families, we are a generation jaded by marital failure. But when I get right down to it, I—like so many in my generation— secretly desire a great, fulfilling, lifelong marriage, only I've been too petrified to even try. What if I make a mistake?

All that said, adventures with Mat had never failed to teach me something before. And while it seemed far-fetched that I would meet Ms. Right while scouring retirement centers for happily married geriatrics, I did see this excursion as a golden opportunity to impress women. How adorable I'd seem, a single guy traveling the country interviewing *When Harry Met Sally* couples! Hearing that, girls could draw their own conclusions about my desire to settle down, and then we'd make out for a while.

"Count me in," I told Mat.

We put a map and an itinerary on the wall: twenty-five major cities all across the United States, twelve thousand miles on the road in a giant RV—all in just nine weeks. "Project Everlasting: The Search for America's Greatest Marriages," we called it, giving each other a big high five in celebration of our daring ingenuity.

And that's when crazy things began to happen. Before we knew it, our little adventure landed us on national television, with sponsors who believed in the work we were about to do, and thousands of applications came pouring in from couples wanting to be part of Project Everlasting. We hit the road.

From a cattle ranch in Oregon to a dance club in a Manhattan skyscraper, we scoured the country in search of Marriage Masters, asking our generation's toughest relationship questions.

What I thought would be a five- or six-month lark turned into the most meaningful, eye-opening four years of my life. I was amazed at how wrong I'd been about the older generation. Certainly, we met couples that stayed together out of convention or convenience and bicker like nobody's business, but this only enhanced our education in matrimony. We were able to determine what the amazing couples are doing to set themselves apart from the ho-hum couples, the couples who are just trying to get by. The couples who inspired us run their marriages on a foundation of respect, commitment, and sharing, and if that sounds old-fashioned, consider that upholding those values has also kept their romance alive decade after decade and allowed them to live contentedly with quirks and habits that would easily—and probably unnecessarily—drive modern couples apart.

Regardless of their age, people are people, and relationships are not era specific. Irritations, in-laws, income issues, and insecurities—all the elements that can strain a marriage—haven't actually changed all that much over the years. Likewise, the principles for success these couples shared with us are timeless. They don't rust, wear out, or run dry. Mark Twain put it best: "Love seems the swiftest, but it is the slowest of all growths. No man or woman really knows what perfect love is until they have been married a quarter of a century."

No matter how differently Mat and I approached this project in the beginning, after interviewing more than 250 Marriage Masters, we've both come to the same conclusion: Our elders' wisdom has the power to shift hearts and change lives. Looking at the positive sea change in our personal understandings of love and marriage, we accepted the responsibility we'd been given from these inspirational couples: We would share their message, their legacy of lifelong love, with those who desire the same. This is why we've written *Project Everlasting:* to increase the love in the world, one couple at a time.

This book is a result of the fifteen thousand combined years of devoted marriage. We are grateful for these couples' willingness to share their wisdom, sincerity, and vulnerability. Some of them drove hours to share their stories with us. "I hope our story helps someone out there find the joy that our marriage has given us," one couple said.

Einstein said that a mind introduced to a new idea never returns to the same size. After four years of Project Everlasting, Mat and I now know that Einstein's principle applies to the heart as well. The Marriage Masters leave a legacy of love that has already expanded our hearts. We sincerely hope that their message moves and expands your heart as well.

Chapter 1

How Did You Know You'd Found the One?

SOUL MATE AT THE MAGAZINE STAND

—by Jason

After months of talking about it and researching, planning, and preparing for it, we were finally packed up and getting on the road for the adventure of our lives: The Search for America's Greatest Marriages.

As we pulled out of our Los Angeles neighborhood, Mat and I beamed at each other, our faces supercharged with excitement. I'd already taken Mat by the shoulders and shouted, "We're really doing it though, huh, Boggsie?"—and it was all I could do to suppress the sudden urge to do it again. We were like Harry and Lloyd of *Dumb and Dumber* on their way up to Aspen, only instead of clinging to each other on a minibike, we were traveling

in a living room on wheels. Our wise chief navigator and in-house Marriage Master, Grandma Dorothy, suggested that we stop and get some reading materials for the road. (Little did we know that we would scarcely have time to sleep during the ensuing nine weeks, let alone kick back with some leisure reading.) So, a full two and a half miles into our nationwide tour, we made our first stop: the local bookstore.

Inside, I was busy scanning the shelves for some serious literature, maybe some Faulkner, or Dostoevsky, or, ahem, I'd always heard a lot of positive things about that one research book covering the fifty best places to kiss in America, too. Just when I'd found Niagara Falls, Mat came whipping around the corner, a little short of breath.

"Talk about serendipitous," Mat said to me with a weighty, self-assured nod. "I think I've found her."

"Who?" I scanned the bookstore for serendipitous females. "Where?"

"I haven't talked to her yet, but she's incredible." He gazed longingly across the great expanse of bookshelves to the magazine racks. "She could be the one."

Since the third grade, I'd witnessed at least a hundred of Mat's "I think I've found the one" events, but it's still always a worthwhile adventure to watch him "Boggsenate" his wives-to-be. "Need a wingman?" I asked.

"Follow me," he beckoned.

As we wended our way toward Mat's new goddess, I took a moment to admire my boy's semiridiculous ambition. It's not his desire to find his wife that I found amusing—don't we all sort of think we might want to meet that special someone maybe within the next five or ten years? It's more his mad obsession for re-creating scenes from movies like *Serendipity* and *Before Sunrise* in his romantic life. Run-of-the-mill "we met at a party" or "a mutual friend hooked us up" encounters won't do for Mat. He needs to bump into her at the top of Mt. Everest. He needs crazy circumstances and magical coincidences. He needs stars to collide. Mat needs more than a wife; he needs a bona fide love story.

As we approached, I watched him secretly record a mental Rembrandt of her, maybe with soft, fluorescent bookstore lights bouncing off her dark hair, her eyes exuding innocence and passion at the same time, and so forth. The way he figures, their grandkids are going to appreciate these kinds of details.

"Oh. My. God," Mat exalted. "There she is . . ."

I had to admit, she was a dandy, a total Boggsie girl. Her skin was smooth, her makeup picture-perfect. She had a certain glow about her; she had plenty of teeth. And though she seemed a little on the quiet side for Mat, I could understand how that face alone would entice him to pick her up and pay the $5.95 cover price.

"This is my soul mate. This is a cosmic connection," he said with absolute conviction, tapping the cover of the March issue of *Bride & Groom* magazine. "I've *got* to find her."

The hopelessly impractical love dork who is my best friend likes to fall in love with beauty first. And second. In close third, she must smell delicious. I mean mouth-watering, I-just-smeared-five-bottles-of-Victoria's-Secret-lotion-all-over-my-body-for-you delicious. Sure, most of us put some degree of priority on the attraction factor, but sensational beauty is the sun, the moon, and the stars in Mat's relationship universe.

For the purposes of always having someone pretty to look at over dinner, or having someone with a delicious smell to cuddle up next to for a movie on the couch, his strategy tends to work really well. His girlfriends from years gone by could all get together and do a photo shoot for a new calendar called "Twelve Months of Women Wearing Layer After Layer of Homely, Frumpish Wool Sweaters" and it would instantly put *Sports Illustrated*'s swimsuit series out of business. I'd be first in line, actually.

Relationships that survive past opening the magazine, however, are nowhere to be seen with Mat Boggs.

For the purposes of long-term relationships, where the full spectrum of one's character is flushed out and explored, Mat's beauty-first strategy hasn't served well. The Band-Aid that beauty provides falls off after about three months, at which point he realizes that attraction is not synonymous with compatibility. He gets confused, wonders why things aren't exciting or enjoyable anymore, then launches a surprise attack breakup on her. She never sees it coming and she never knows why he's breaking up with her—he doesn't either, just that, "I wasn't feeling it anymore." A few weeks later, after thorough analysis, he deduces that the woman simply wasn't the One in the first place, which can mean only that the One must still be out there, still patiently swimming in the sweet syrups of serendipity, still waiting for Mat to stumble into the pool alongside her. And the pattern carries on—it's a vicious, vixen cycle.

If Mat's relationship logic is slightly impaired, I'm just plain stupid. If my highest priority in a wife-to-be isn't beauty—and that's debatable—then it's the woman's spelling abilities. Yeah, that's right, spelling. Mat digs the smelling; I get turned on by the girl who knows that *definately* is definitely not a word in the English language.

My strategy for finding this beautiful Queen of *Webster's* is pretty much indecipherable. Rather than the standard, more proactive approach of asking a woman out for a date, I'd rather she come to me. Not that I'm lying around like a lazy Venus flytrap. No, I put a lot of effort into crafting creative bait, like the time I created the "Adventures with Bunnie Wuv" cartoon series, or hypothetical romantic scenes on my blog.

The way I see it, some lovely girl is going to take the bait because she gets me, and respond accordingly. Meaning, she'll email me—spelling airtight—and we'll get married. So far, my strategy hasn't been as productive as I'd hoped.

Really, is it any wonder that Mat and I are still bachelors?

Actually, the Marriage Masters did wonder. After getting riddled with my marital questions, many of my interviewees felt compelled to poke around a bit into my personal relationship story.

"Do you have a special woman in your life, Jason?"

"Nope. As single as single gets."

"How old are you, son?"

"Twenty-eight."

"I don't get it. You seem to have a good head on your shoulders. You're tall. Why aren't you married yet?"

"Well, I've been trying for a while now, but the problem is . . . [insert Scapegoat of the Month here]."

Mat's favorite excuse was, "I'm too busy learning about marriage to get married," whereas I took the more self-righteous route: "There just don't seem to be any women who value commitment these days!"

Right. We can only hope the interviewees were more sincere with their answers.

The truth of the matter is that we've both been in relationships with women who fit every criterion we've been supposedly holding out for—relationships we just *knew* would go the distance. But we fumbled the ball. Which brings up the lesson I've learned about *How do I know when I've met The One?* It really doesn't matter *how* you meet The One. One couple got engaged the first night they met—the cosmic connection type; the next waited five years to analyze the relationship from every possible angle. There is no one formula for success.

So the answers we got were all over the board, and guess what? They were all good. However, we did hear some themes about how couples came to the realization.

Like, look for someone who has the same value system, especially in regard to family and money. If you value family time first and foremost and your wife's way more fascinated with making a lot of money, then there are going to be some major problems. Likewise, if your dream is one day to play ball with little Trevor in the backyard and your husband is dreading the nightmare of little Trevor ruining his peaceful life and household, things may get ugly. The Marriage Masters were all for discussing individual priority systems before saying "I do"—some of them learned the importance of this the hard way.

And, marry someone of the same religion or spiritual beliefs if religion is very important to you. It may seem unnecessary when you first get married—it doesn't seem like a big deal to accept one another's perspectives even if they are different from your own. But then you have kids. Interfaith marriages certainly aren't doomed—we met many Marriage Masters who started out with different belief systems and still made it—but it seemed at some point it had been the thorn in their marriage's side and a major bone of contention. More often than not, one of them eventually switched over to the other's religion to solve the problem.

We've all heard it a thousand times, especially from our moms: Beauty isn't everything. And yet it remains at the top of the list. I don't know if there's a nice way to put this, but . . . hundreds of interviews with people who've passed their physical prime are the best reminder: Beauty is most definitely not everything. Some grandmas and grandpas get more handsome as time goes by, but most do not. So what takes the place of beauty as gravity starts to work its wonders on our bodies? Friendship. Find a person who makes you laugh. Someone with whom you can talk for hours on end. Someone with whom you feel utterly comfortable sharing yourself. Someone whom you know would love you even at your ugliest. Someone whose mind is just as attractive as his or her booty. Someone with whom you share common interests. Someone you can trust with your life. That kind of friend.

As for my cosmically connected counterpart, two months after pointing out his cover girl in the Los Angeles bookstore, we walked into to Doris Elmer's Oregon home to do an interview, and wouldn't you know it? There's the same magazine sitting on her coffee table.

"Hey, there's my girl!" he says to me. "What a coincidence, huh?"

You can imagine my surprise when Doris piped up, "Oh, yes, that's my granddaughter. Isn't she beautiful?" Before Mat could mentally begin writing the script for his real-life remake of *Serendipity,* Doris broke the bad news: "Sorry, she's engaged."

And so while we continue our search, here are three couples who found exactly what they were looking for more than forty years ago.

> ## *Found in Translation*
> Martha and Argyl Schildnecht
> Married 57 years

The first time Martha saw her future husband, she thought he looked like a movie star—just not her favorite one. This was Hollywood 1949, and the fellow standing in the apartment doorway with a big smile and rugged profile was more a Hugh Downs type, nicely dressed in a brown suit and tie, handsome, really, but no Clark Gable.

For his part, Argyl felt something tug at his heart the moment he saw Martha in her green silk sheath, a petticoat peeking out just below the knee. She wore a leopard-skin jacket. Her eyes were dark and exotic, as if she belonged to another world. "She's something!" he thought. Then she said "Hello," not one word more, and Argyl thought, "What a stuck-up woman!" At the time, he had no idea that Martha spoke not one word of English beyond "hello." He was also unaware that this visitor from Mexico City had come to California to pick out a trousseau for her marriage to another man, that she had only recently broken the engagement, and most certainly he did not know that she had agreed to the evening in the sole hope that their itinerary might include driving by homes where the movie stars lived.

Not the most auspicious beginning for fifty-plus years of wedded bliss, but as blind dates go, it wasn't off to a bad start.

Martha, twenty-one, had been engaged to Fernando, a few years her senior. They shared a similar background. In Mexico City, Martha's mother employed two maids who changed sheets, ironed clothes, served food, even brought Martha a glass of chilled water while she practiced the piano. Fernando's father, who was even more well off, had already decreed that the newlyweds would live in his mansion. Both father and son were proud of Martha's musical talent, but when the young woman confessed her dream of one day becoming a concert pianist, Fernando told her, "Forget that."

Then a family friend invited Martha and her mother, Refugio, to visit Los Angeles and select a trousseau. She promised that the young bride-to-be would have the time of her life shopping for dresses and lingerie in Beverly Hills. Martha couldn't wait.

During one afternoon of shopping, Martha realized that the clothes excited her more than the marriage. Fernando had already picked out their linens and had them embroidered. Martha didn't get to choose so much as a stitch. She'd met an American couple who were engaged and marveled at how the man and woman made decisions together. Martha suddenly knew what love was, and what it was not. "What am I doing? I'm not in love with this man," she thought. She couldn't spend the rest of her life bossed around by a man with whom she shared only upbringing. After getting her mother's approval, off went a telegram to Mexico City the very next day.

Argyl was nothing like Martha's former fiancé. He let others do the talking. His Spanish rivaled Martha's English. A Missouri native, he'd been enticed to Los Angeles by his old friend Burl. Argyl arrived in LA with $20 in his pocket and soon found work on the assembly line at General Motors in Long Beach. Burl's girlfriend, Dora, lived in the apartment complex where Martha was staying. Burl and Dora planned a double date, but somehow the matchmakers neglected to tell their friends that neither spoke the other's language. After Martha said "hello" to him and nothing more, Dora, who was bilingual, stepped in to interpret. Argyl realized his date didn't have "a chip on her shoulder" after all. But how on earth would they get through the evening if they couldn't manage a simple conversation?

The foursome headed out to the tropical-themed Zamboanga Club off the Sunset Strip. A talker by nature, Martha got antsy sitting quietly on the ride over. How she longed to chatter away like she always did! But how could she? "Wait a minute," she thought. "I know just what to do." She would fill the void with a beloved custom from back home, one adhered to on buses, trains, and cars. Without any preamble, Martha burst into song. Her rich voice filled the vehicle, and she sang Mexican favorites all the way to the club. A startled Argyl sat in silence. "Not like the girls in Missouri," he thought. "Not at all."

At the same time, he couldn't help being enchanted by the sound of his date's voice, even if he couldn't understand a word. Never had he known a woman so at ease with herself, so bold and full of life. "That's a pretty exotic gal," he told himself.

The club also caught Argyl unawares, with its South Seas theme and crowd of swaying, loose-limbed dancers. "Wait a minute! I'm a square-dancing kind of guy," he thought. Come rumba time, Martha led. Argyl was stunned. He thought, "This is one strong-willed lady." And yet he had no desire to let go of the woman in his arms, even as he stumbled and stepped on her feet.

On the ride home, Argyl casually rested his hand on Martha's leg, which earned him a slap. For that, Argyl didn't need an interpreter.

Argyl spent the next week showing Martha the sights with Dora interpreting and Martha's mother chaperoning. They visited Malibu Beach, Grauman's Chinese Theatre, and, map in hand, toured the streets inhabited by Hollywood stars. "Here I am breathing the same air as the movie stars," she kept telling herself.

The following week, Martha and Argyl, Dora and Burl, Martha's mother, and a group of other friends headed south to San Diego. They ate lunch at the beautiful Rosarito Beach Hotel in Baja, overlooking the ocean, while an orchestra played in the dining room. When the orchestra took a break, Martha's friends urged her toward the piano. When Martha played the classical tango "Jealousy," Argyl thought, "She's amazing." When the diners burst into applause, he felt tremendous pride that this talented, beautiful woman was his. But for how long? In a few weeks, she would return to Mexico, where Fernando was surely waiting. After all, what man would let a woman like this get away?

The next day, the group stopped in La Jolla before heading back to Los Angeles. At a park overlooking the ocean, Argyl spread out a blanket for him and Martha, keeping a respectful distance between them. He didn't want Martha to go home. But what could he do? Argyl had gotten into the habit of keeping a small spiral notebook in his jacket pocket. Sitting there on the blanket, he took out the notebook and a pencil and began to sketch.

Sunlight glinted off the water, making the waves sparkle, and Martha thought, "Isn't that nice, he's sketching the ocean," but Argyl's drawing didn't look like any beach she'd ever seen. There was a cross. It looked like . . . a church?

Argyl was following an instinct he did not entirely understand. Up until now, he had planned to marry at thirty-two, that is, not for another eight years. At that age, a man would have achieved financial stability, he figured. And while Argyl had never envisioned the specifics of his marriage proposal, he was fairly certain it did not include an interpreter. "We'll see what happens here," he thought. Argyl drew a woman. A veil cascaded from her head. Fingers clutched a bouquet. Next he drew a man wearing a tuxedo. Argyl's heart was pounding so loudly he could barely hear the ocean. "I hope she understands," he told himself.

Argyl pointed to the bride, then to Martha. "She looks a little perplexed," he thought. He took a deep breath. He pointed to the groom, then to himself. He turned to Martha. Would she accept his proposal?

Martha couldn't help herself. She burst out laughing. "This guy is crazy!" she thought.

But Argyl refused to be dissuaded. He instructed Dora: "Let Martha's mother know, I'll be asking for her daughter's hand in marriage. And soon." The next night, on bended knee, Argyl approached Refugio while Maria, another bilingual friend, interpreted. Refugio didn't see the need to rush things. Martha should go home to Mexico and she and Argyl could write each other. Argyl, usually so agreeable, refused. He couldn't bear to be away from Martha, and he didn't trust that Fernando.

Ultimately, Maria persuaded Refugio that her daughter would be treated like a princess and painted for Martha a Technicolor picture of American marriage. "You'll go dancing every weekend," Maria assured her. Envisioning her life as something out of the movies, Martha said yes.

A week later, before ten guests, Martha and Argyl became man and wife. The bilingual priest turned to Martha, then Argyl, alternately conducting the ceremony in Spanish and English.

Two days later, Martha returned to Mexico to renew her visa, and Argyl went apartment hunting in Los Angeles. In a letter, he described the wonderful home he had found, and Martha's friend in Mexico City translated. "He says it is a very nice apartment, with a living room, dining room, bedroom, and a dressing room," the friend told her. Martha couldn't wait to begin her new life.

Before carrying his bride across the threshold, Argyl told Martha to close her eyes.

When she opened them, she couldn't believe it. "This is where I'm going to live?" she thought. "Oh, dear."

The luxurious dwelling turned out to be a small studio with an old sofa and chair in one corner, and a bed with no headboard in another. Martha had never seen a bed without a headboard before. A few feet from the bed stood a little round table—apparently this was the dining room. Martha peered out the kitchen window to a dark alley, where a Dumpster overflowed with bags of trash.

She couldn't help but remember her home in Mexico City, where each night the maid turned down Martha's bed and left a fresh glass of water on the nightstand. She had never done housework. Martha's first attempt at ironing left her in tears; she couldn't get the wrinkles out of her husband's blue jeans. Without a live-in interpreter, conversation was sparse. Martha's movie-life fantasy dissolved before her eyes.

And yet, she also saw that she had married a good man. Soon, she stopped missing the luxuries she'd once taken for granted. Argyl marveled at the gourmet soups she whipped up from leftover chicken and tomatoes. On Sundays the couple picnicked in the park and splurged on a 35¢ double feature. Argyl was sweet, kind, and patient. He loved her completely. He helped with the ironing. Once, she decided to surprise her husband by baking an elaborate cake. The recipe called for cornstarch, and Martha, whose English was still shaky, used laundry starch instead. Come time to cut the cake, Argyl couldn't get a knife through the starched confection. "Don't worry," he told her, and pronounced her creation beautiful. That whole first year of marriage, he carried Martha over the threshold every day.

Martha felt profoundly loved. The sight of her husband's face first thing every morning filled her with an unfathomable joy. Unlike Argyl, there was never a moment that Martha suddenly realized, "Yes, he is the one!" Instead, she had a growing awareness of her happiness, that the man to whom she had committed for life had become her life.

Nearly six decades later, the two still tease each other about that first date, when Argyl felt Martha should have been more cordial. "What did you want me to do, go with open arms, embrace you and say, 'Hello, my American man!'?" She laughs.

"I got married for all the wrong reasons," Martha admits, as she snuggles next to Argyl. "This situation was very wild and I

told my kids I would kill them if they did the same thing. But we had love on our side, and although we couldn't speak the same language, we had a love communication between us."

When asked how he knew Martha was the one for him, Argyl replies, "There was something that clicked with Martha. I saw her and *bang!*, I knew. When it hits you it hits you. Luckily, I ended up falling in love with her culture, her family values, and her beliefs, too."

"Jealousy," the song Martha played at the Rosarito Beach Hotel, became their song. Martha likes to play the CD, and the two of them dance in the living room. Martha still likes to lead. Argyl doesn't mind.

Sometimes, Martha teasingly asks her husband, "Why do you love me so much?"

"Because you're unique," he says.

"You don't want somebody quiet and proper?"

"No, I like you just the way you are."

As for Martha? She wouldn't trade her husband for all the Clark Gables in the world.

The Runaround Romance

Bud and June Hodge
Married 51 years

Night had fallen by the time Bud arrived at his cousin's home in Walnut Creek, California. After five hours on the road, he was eager to take a dip in the backyard pool. Opening the slider, he saw that the pool lights had turned the water a luminescent blue and cast a hazy halo on the lone female figure gliding underwater toward the deep end. "That's my friend June," his cousin explained.

Bud didn't hesitate. "What a cute little body," he thought and dove in after her. The two nearly knocked heads. Bud, who always swam with his eyes open, could just make out, through the rippling water, a pretty face with a startled expression.

June felt a tremendous splash but couldn't see much. She rose to the surface, thinking, "What the heck is going. . . . Oh. He's cute. *Very* cute."

"Hello," she said, "and who are you?"

They spent a pleasant evening sipping Cokes and snacking on pretzels by the pool. Bud's cousin Sandra was June's best friend. "You don't want to get involved with him," Sandra warned. "He's got a lot of girls on a string." June shrugged. No problem. After all, Bud, twenty, was on a Liberty Pass from the U.S. naval station far away in San Diego, while June would be a junior at Acalanes High in Lafayette that fall. She'd probably never even see the guy again.

Two years later, Bud was back visiting cousin Sandra in Northern California. "By the way, June's coming with us to the movies tonight," Sandra told him. That sounded good to Bud. Every now and then, he'd thought about that five-foot bundle of energy, but she'd been just a kid and he'd been busy admiring San Diego's many attractions, particularly the young female variety. June seemed more grown up now, having just graduated from high school, but their night at the movies didn't feel like a date to him, not with cousin Sandra, a self-appointed chaperone.

That fall, June entered UC Berkeley and Bud got his orders.

He was shipping out for the Far East. For his last weekend of freedom, he decided to head north and suggested a double date, perhaps dinner and dancing at the Officers' Club in Alameda. "How about I take that girl, June? Think you could get her number for me?" Bud asked Sandra.

Bud couldn't take his eyes off June all evening. She was so bubbly and vivacious. When they danced, holding her in his arms felt like the most natural thing in the world, even though Bud was more than a foot taller than his date, and June stepped on his feet every now and then. Everything Bud said made her laugh. She couldn't believe how much fun she was having now that she was in college, and in a sorority, too! Here she was tonight, on her eighteenth birthday, in a grown-up Officers' Club with this handsome man in his sport jacket and pressed slacks. Wait until she told her sorority sisters!

Bud took June back to her sorority house and kissed her good night. The kiss curled his toes.

"You know, I'm shipping out tomorrow," Bud reminded her. "I'd like to write you, if that's okay."

"Sure," said June, thinking, "Why not?"

Aboard the USS *Montague*, third-class personnel man Bud Hodge managed the ship's log and bunked in the office. Every evening, after completing the log, he put a fresh sheet of paper in the typewriter and began: *"Dear June: Today we crossed the international date line. I am working very hard. . . ."* Or *"Dear June: Today we saw a show. . . . Looking forward to hearing from you."* At first, he debated over the proper closing sentiment, then thought, "You gotta start somewhere," and signed each letter, *"Love, Bud."* The voyage to Japan took eighteen days, and since Bud wrote June every day, he had accumulated an impressive stack of envelopes by the time the *Montague* pulled into the Japanese harbor. He wondered briefly if the entire batch would arrive at June's sorority on the same day, and if she might be at all taken aback by the sheer volume of correspondence. But no, he and June had something going. Memories of their kiss on the threshold of the Alpha Omicron Pi house had seen him through many a lonely night at sea. He kept on writing to his college girl.

In high school, Berkeley had been June's dream. Now she was living it. Only the second person on either side of the family to attend college—the first had been her sister—June threw herself into college life with gusto. She made the honor roll and received a scholarship award. The sorority named her Outstanding Pledge. She became an editor at Berkeley's monthly magazine, joined the Pep Club, and sang in the a capella choir. Then there was dating. Often, June had a different date each weekend. From time to time, she'd walk into her sorority house after a long day at school, arms loaded with books, and there would be a letter from Bud, the cute fellow from the navy she'd gone out with that one time. "Isn't that nice," she'd tell herself, reading the contents. Should she dash off a note? "Oh, not right now." June sighed. She loathed writing letters. Besides, she had an English paper due. And a pep rally that weekend. So many exciting things were happening at school, who could think of anything else?

After five months at sea, Bud had received many letters from his parents and his friends, but he never once heard from

June. "I guess that's the end of it," Bud thought. And he put her out of his mind. Really, he did.

Bud returned to the States after fifteen months overseas. He enrolled at the University of Nevada in Reno, not far from his parents' dairy ranch. One weekend, he came home to do laundry and stock up on food. He was in the kitchen, rifling through the refrigerator, when his mother, Birdie, said, "Buddy, there's a letter here from June Derry."

"Oh, really." Bud took the envelope, opened the cupboard beneath the kitchen sink, and threw the letter in the trash.

"Whoa! Wait a minute there," said Birdie. "Aren't you even going to open it?

"No way."

"That's not how I raised you," his mother told him. "Good, bad, or indifferent, you open that letter. You read it. And you respond to it."

The letter was an invitation. Would Bud like to take June to her sorority's spring formal?

"No way," Bud thought. Yet he found himself writing back and accepting the invitation. He packed up his best black pin-striped suit and red tie. On the five-hour drive to Berkeley, Bud was apprehensive and a little angry. "Dad-gam-it! Why am I doing this? She never responded." Bud pulled into town, stopping at a florist. He bought the prettiest corsage he could find. "Why'd she ask me to come to this thing? What's her motive?" he continued to wonder as he pulled up to the sorority house.

Bud caught his breath. June looked stunning, even prettier than he remembered. She was as warm and bubbly as ever. At the dance that night, Bud told her about Guam, Okinawa, Vietnam, and Korea. June blushed as she told Bud about being crowned "Soph Doll." College fraternities throughout California had elected June winner of a talent and beauty contest. Bud and June laughed and talked all evening. They talked about sports, school, the Korean War. But they never once talked about the mail. They kissed good night. Bud's toes curled. Again.

Bud practically floated back to Reno. " 'Soph Doll!' Not like she couldn't get a date!" thought Bud. "She didn't have to import a fellow from another state." Unless . . . unless . . . Bud did mean something to her, after all.

After their date, June was glad that she'd followed through on her whim to take Bud to the dance. When her best friend Sandra had mentioned, "Did you know my cousin Bud's back from overseas?" June thought, "I wonder if he'd like to come down for a sorority formal?" The dance had been fun. It was nice seeing Bud again. He seemed more mature than the college boys she dated.

Bud wrote June. She did not write back.

"What in heck is going on here?" Bud thought. "I can't believe she got me again." He enrolled in summer school and began dating a young woman who had the added attraction of proximity even if her kisses left his toes indifferent. Then one day, June called him. "Will wonders never cease?" he thought.

"My parents are renting a place in Lake Tahoe for a week," she told him. "Why don't you join us?" June's parents liked Bud. They had gotten to know him through Sandra's parents. June didn't understand what had prompted her sudden invitation, or even why she had asked him to that sorority dance when he lived so far away. His letters, of which she recalled receiving only a handful, had been sweet, but honestly, she hadn't paid them much attention. Still, when it came time for June to choose a companion, for some reason she kept choosing Bud.

"Would you like to go?" she repeated.

"I'm a fool," Bud thought. "A fool." He said, "Sure."

The week in Tahoe was magic. Bud marveled at June's kindness. "I bet she's never said a bad word about anyone," he thought. Bud considered himself judgmental and found that being around June made him more open-minded. June admired Bud's maturity, his respect for her parents, and how he made her laugh all day long.

So when Bud said, "Why don't you come spend a week on my family's dairy ranch next month?" June didn't hesitate. But no sooner did June arrive than Birdie had to leave town on a family emergency. Bud and his dad wondered if June might take over with the cooking, explaining that they had four ranch hands to feed. Although she'd never cooked before, she cheerfully agreed.

Bud's dad, Leon, gently suggested she cook some steaks. "Surely she can't mess up steaks," he whispered to his son. June didn't let on that her entire experience with an oven consisted of baking chocolate chip cookies. The broil setting was a mystery. Sitting across the table from her, trying to saw through his raw-in-the-middle blackened fillet, Bud thought June had never looked more adorable.

A few evenings later, under the big cottonwood tree out near the field, Bud presented June with his fraternity pin. A few minutes later, he got down on one knee. "I love you," he said. "Will you marry me?" June said "Yes!" right away. After being together five times in four years, "I finally got swept off my feet," June said. They married four months later, on December 23, 1955.

Married life was hard at first. Bud attended school on the GI Bill, and the couple could not afford health insurance when June became pregnant. Plus, there were personality differences to reconcile between strong-willed Bud and shier, easygoing June. "Everybody has situations to work through," she said. "But we had made a commitment. There was never a time I thought, 'I'm not going to stay with this.' It wasn't even a question. Bud is the one for me."

Being married to June makes Bud feel like the luckiest man in the world. In 1972, the couple started an industrial equipment company with $500 and a used station wagon. June did the books and packed a week's worth of sandwiches in a cooler for Bud to eat on the road. He slept in the wagon and washed up at gas stations. Together, they created and nurtured what would become an $18 million enterprise. The two share many interests, including golfing, dancing, travel, and music. June plans lavish charity functions at their country club, where both parties agree: They've each got the best-looking escort.

"No matter what happened, Bud kept coming back into my life. I don't think that was a coincidence. I followed my instincts. I envisioned an always-and-forever marriage, a lifetime commitment with children—a real family. I wanted love, friendship, fun, and a partner who could be all of this. And boy, did I ever choose right!"

Bud doesn't really understand what made him literally go far out of his way, way back then, for a girl who didn't seem particularly interested, only that something in his heart said, "Do not give up." He's glad he followed his instinct. Around June, Bud felt "so comfortable, at ease, and understood." Over time, "I knew she would become my best friend, companion, and wife for the rest of my life."

What it really boils down to, he said, "She's the only one who made my toes curl. She still does."

There's just one thing Bud still doesn't understand: "Why in heck didn't she answer my letters?" Then he laughs. Every marriage, he says, even one spanning more than half a century, still needs a bit of mystery.

> ## *No Holds Barred*
> **Willem and Vera Wormer**
> **Married 58 years**

Jakarta, Indonesia, 1945. No one dared scale the bamboo fence. Sharpened stakes fifteen feet tall bound with bamboo wire sharp enough to shred a man's hands and feet discouraged escape as effectively as a spear-wielding sentry. What further booby traps awaited them on the other side, the detainees had no idea.

Why take such a risk, anyway? The life they'd known beyond the fence no longer existed. Since the Japanese seized control of the Dutch East Indies in 1942, men, women, and children of European descent had been rounded up and placed in camps, their homes and possessions confiscated.

So none of the 150 young men inside Camp Menteng Pulo ever talked about escape, including Willem Wormer. But Willem thought of little else. On the other side of the fence, three miles down the road, lived a Spice Islands beauty named Vera whom Willem adored.

They'd met in 1944, before his parents, brothers, and sisters had been scattered to different camps. Vera's cousin had invited Willem over for badminton, and the eighteen-year-old was instantly smitten with the dignified twenty-three-year-old teacher. "An older woman," he thought. "I haven't got a chance."

At first, Vera kept her distance on the other side of the net, but Willem's gallant persistence won out. Unfailingly polite, he always arrived at her door with some gift, usually flowers, and he treated her mother respectfully. "So different from those other boys," Vera thought. For her birthday, he presented her with a delicate orchid.

Dating was difficult in Batavia (now Jakarta) under the Japanese occupation, but still Willem loved to tempt fate by getting Vera home just before curfew struck at 10 P.M. Although Vera was of mixed race and raised in the Dutch tradition, the Japanese considered her family Asian and left them alone.

On the other hand, Willem, being half Dutch, was targeted by the secret police. One night, they picked him up and gave him a choice: Work with us, or be sent to the camps. "No, I don't want to collaborate," he told them. In early 1945, Willem found himself on a former pig and cow farm on the edge of town now barricaded by bamboo.

Still, Willem considered himself lucky. This camp, run by Dutch collaborators, was not like the notorious women's and children's Tjideng Camp known as "Hell on Earth," or other Japanese-run camps where his friends died of hunger or beatings. Menteng Pulo was a brutal place nonetheless—food was scarce and lice were rampant.

After four months of living on watery soup, rice, and the occasional purloined tomato root, Willem felt he would never be full again. He fantasized about chicken in hot-pepper sauce and co-

conut milk. But the pain in his heart was even greater than the ache in his gut. Willem's head swam with visions of Vera. "How can I see her again?" he kept asking himself.

Like the other prisoners, Willem had come through a guarded entrance at one end of camp and had no idea what type of spiked deterrent awaited him outside his barracks at the other end. The fence was as dense as a stone wall. But one day, Willem noticed a tiny slit between two bamboo poles and pressed his eye to the opening. Yes! He saw no bamboo spears, only grass and sand. He got an idea, sharing his plan with no one. But such a thing had never been tried. It was impossible, wasn't it? A week later, he told himself, "The hell with it, I'm going."

That night, when no one was looking, he climbed the fence's horizontal reinforcement beams like steps on a ladder, never mind they were three feet apart. Willem didn't think about being beaten or killed if he got caught. He didn't worry about losing his flimsy rubber sandals or ripping his skin on the wire. He didn't even stop to consider that the narrow strip of grass he'd spied through the slats might not accurately represent the full landscape.

"I have to see Vera," he thought and plunged into the inky darkness.

Landing like a cat on all fours in a patch of sand, Willem ran as fast as he could all the way to Vera's house.

Vera was so stunned, her mouth fell open. "How did you . . . ?" she started to ask, but Willem cut her off with a hug.

Finally she asked, "Did you get permission?"

"No, I jumped the fence."

Vera was silent. "This man is risking his life for me!" she

thought. But she couldn't bear the danger. "You shouldn't have come," she said. "I don't know what they'll do to you if you're caught. Don't do this anymore."

All the while Vera's mother heaped one bowl of food after another in front of her starving guest.

Willem stayed only thirty minutes. If he remained out after curfew, the Japanese patrols would surely spot him. Vera walked him outside, and the two kissed good-bye. "Be careful!" she called after him, wondering if she would ever see Willem again.

He raced back to the camp and scaled a shorter but more dangerous wall next to where the Dutch collaborators slept. Willem snuck past the sleeping guards, down to the prisoners' barracks, and slipped silently onto the communal wooden plank that was his bed.

Three weeks later, Willem jumped the fence again.

"I love you," he told a startled Vera. "I had to see you again."

"I love you, too," she replied. "But don't come back. It's too dangerous." It was July 1945, and Vera told him she'd heard the war might soon end.

This time, Willem stayed put in camp.

When the Americans bombed Hiroshima and Nagasaki a few weeks later, forcing a Japanese surrender, Willem's camp was closed and the men inside freed.

A week after obtaining his freedom, Willem confidently proposed to Vera. After all, he'd twice escaped a prison camp just to see her. There could be no doubt as to his devotion. "Don't you think it's time we get married?" he asked.

Vera loved Willem. The man had risked his life for a few stolen moments with her. He treated her and her family with the utmost respect. Deep in her heart, Vera believed she had found the one. Still, Vera was a practical schoolteacher. A heady wartime romance didn't necessarily promise a successful future. "If this marriage is meant to be—and I believe that it is—it can wait," she thought.

She told Willem, "Not yet," adding, "you need to finish school first."

Much to his own surprise, Willem agreed. He knew before he'd even scaled the fence that he wanted to spend the rest of his life with Vera. Willem had had no interest in pursuing a university degree, but if his Vera wanted him to jump yet another hurdle, he would gladly do so. Two years later, he graduated from the university with a bachelor of arts degree.

No sooner did he graduate than Willem was drafted, serving a year as an air traffic controller in the military. Finally, three years after he proposed, Willem married Vera.

Six decades of marriage later, he says, "It was worth the wait."

"Marry someone you respect," Willem says. "She was always a lady. And she was always much wiser than me."

Vera shrugs her shoulders. "What's wise is to find someone who is brave enough to weather the hard times that come in a marriage." Vera looks at Willem in appreciation. "Someone like my husband."

Chapter 2

How Do You Keep from Driving Each Other Nuts?

REFINED TASTE
(OR HOW I LEARNED TO LOSE THE LIST)

— by Mat

From an early age, my parents made it clear to me: "You can achieve anything you want to achieve." All I'd have to do is put my mind to it . . . and be dragged along to a ton of success seminars.

So while most thirteen-year-old kids spent their weekends chasing butterflies and building forts out in the fields, I could be found seated among adults three and four times my age at intimate "reach for the stars" gatherings, learning how to break down the mental and emotional barriers that held us back from excellence. I hated it. I remember sitting cross-legged on the floor, face-to-face with a fifty-something man for a process called "I am _____." For what seemed an eternity, the stranger and I stared into each other's eyes and shared our deepest feelings. "I am awkward," was the only thought going through my head, but that would have been only an average response. I was there to become great. So he consoled me while I told him how badly it hurt when my cheerleader girlfriend dumped me for another guy, and I consoled him as he wept over his impending divorce. Over time, I learned to like these gigs. They made me feel closer to perfection.

Lately, I am perpetually single.

"What I want you all to do right now," said one seminar leader, "is to visualize in your mind what your perfect partner is like, inside and out, every facet. Then I want you to make a list of each quality. Be as specific as possible."

By this time, I was in my early twenties, already well on my way to self-help guruship. I immediately readied my pen and pad, impatient to begin the process of visualizing my wife. I was excited because I knew it would work. Visualization techniques had always been my secret weapon for peak performances in football. In fact, I silently admonished myself for not thinking of this route earlier. *She could have been in your life by now, dummy, maybe even having our first kid.*

With fervent zeal, I launched into my list: *Smart, gorgeous, deeply spiritual, athletic, generous, kind, romantic spirit, laughs at my jokes, calming presence, lives within twenty miles of me, 5'6", brown eyes, likes to paint, loves music, appreciates goofy movies, loves working out, dances really really well, loves football and snowboarding and surfing and decorating for holidays and . . .* Within five minutes my dream woman had sixty-three qualities. So what if I personally didn't possess more than a third of the qualities? This was all about what I saw in my woman. This was about going for the gold. I knew she would be flawless.

I am impatient.

I also knew it would be only a matter of time before my nightly visualizing processes brought this woman into my life. I taped the list to my bathroom mirror and read it while brushing my teeth. Sure enough, I met her six months later. She was exactly five-six, fun, smart, and spiritual. She had smoldering brown eyes, perfect skin, and gorgeous, silky hair. She liked football enough. Oh, and she was breathtakingly, stunningly, hauntingly beautiful. I mean *smoking*. I fell in love quickly.

Just as quickly I figured out the secret behind her breathtaking, stunning, haunting, smoking beauty: a *really* long time in the bathroom. Her "getting ready" became my cue to get ready for two hours of thumb twirling on the couch. She had to straighten her hair, curl her hair, restraighten her hair, spritz her hair, spray her hair, gel her hair, blow-dry her hair, comb her hair, brush her hair, pluck her hair, put her hair in braids, put her hair up, pull her hair down—*anything* a woman can do to her hair, she had to do it. And that was just the hair! Then it was on to the makeup, and I can't even begin to explain what all of those procedures are called. After that it was the outfit selection, the shoe selection, the accessory selection, the purse selection—but don't get me wrong, the selections were hot. Our relationship's spontaneity, however, was not. If I wanted to see a movie that started in an hour and forty-five minutes—nope, forget about it. "We can be spontaneous," she once told me, "as long as we simply plan ahead." I tried to change her, but she refused to compromise her beauty.

Up went the perfect partner list on the bathroom mirror again. Only this time it had a new item on line 64: *Gorgeous in thirty minutes or less*.

My next girlfriend got ready in ten. Her exotic, expeditious beauty reeled me in, but it was her unparalleled spiritual depths that made me want to stay. At a moment's notice, we could jump in my Jeep and head out to the beach for Dalai Lama-meets-Jesus conversations. We'd lie in the sand for hours on end, staring up into the blue sky and meditating on God and the universe. We pondered the universe. We cracked the code on religion. We decrypted time. Every idea she shared was spiritually mind-expanding for me. I loved it.

That is, until I realized that we could not talk about anything else. She had no off switch for her profound, esoteric magnification of ramification cogitations. I could stay deep in those realms for only so long before I craved a slice of pizza and a cold beer. I tried to teach her how to take time out from discussions about the hunger crises in underdeveloped countries, at least long enough for us to cuddle up together on the recliner with some chips and dips and a Steelers game. I tried to get her to laugh at my jokes and play silly games with me, but she only wanted to paint pictures of spiritual beings in her homemade sanctuary.

Line 65: Deeply spiritual, yet not too serious, and c'mon, able to joke around a bit.

My next girlfriend could have been seen at the Laugh Factory, or on *America's Next Top Model*, or hosting CNN's Headline

News. She's what I called the TFP—total female package: beauty, brains, and gut-busting humor. I loved the way she could cap a poignant conversation with a totally silly, totally adorable joke. Together, we were just two fun-loving dorks who felt completely comfortable being real in each other's presence.

A little too comfortable, actually, because within two months she started to think it was totally adorable to fart around me. I'll admit, I did laugh the first time she did it, but only because I thought it was an accident. But when she started ripping them on a regular basis and literally bending over, touching her toes with her butt in the air while doing it, I did not find her the slightest bit amusing. I tried to get her to stop, but she wouldn't take me seriously.

Line 66: Funny, but not frat house funny.

Three months later, *line 67: Dances really really well, but also chooses the right deodorant.*

Nine months later, line 68: *Sets big goals yet knows to stop and smell the flowers.*

Thirty years later, *line 2,043: Perfect in every way . . . and open to marrying a much older man?*

I am impractical.

The pursuit of perfection defines who I am. I know the cliché: "You won't find the perfect person, just the perfect person for you." I preach it just as much as the next guy. But that "perfect person for you" has been up on my bathroom mirror for a long time now and I'm still not finding her.

"Good luck with that, Mat," my grandma once said. "Even if you do find that pot of gold, you'll find that the gold tarnishes within five years of marriage."

"And it won't take her five weeks to figure out the same of you," added Gramps with a subtle smile. "Take it from me."

I am imperfect.

Gram and Gramps were the first of many elders to instruct me that I'd better get over myself before entering matrimony. Instead of visualizing all the perfections my future wife will have, I should visualize myself overcoming my biggest foible: I am judgmental. When I was faced with a mate's shortcoming, I focused so intensely on the issue that the issue became all I could see. I wanted so badly for it to change, for her to become *a better person,* that I effectually missed the hundreds of great qualities she possessed. It's been a tough lesson for me, but the Marriage Masters promote acceptance or, if possible, gratitude for a mate's annoying personality quirks. Learning to deal with a mate's peccadilloes and idiosyncrasies is just part of the marriage game. No matter how successful the relationship, there are always a handful of annoying habits that drive us nuts about each other. Lord knows that my list of shortcomings is a mile long.

I wasn't totally naïve about all this—I had an inkling there would be a few of these personality thorns in the bed of roses, but I also figured that I could change those imperfections. We'd smooth those thorns out, even if it took a success seminar or two.

No, no, no, the Marriage Masters kept hammering into my brain. "The challenge in marriage, the challenge in love, is not changing our spouse to fit our list. It is changing our list to fit our spouse," one Marriage Master husband put it. "If you think you are going to change the person you married, think again. You'll have enough trouble changing yourself, if that's even possible."

I sat with another couple in Detroit who married after knowing each other only three weeks. Talk about a learning curve in acceptance! The way they described their first year of marriage, their frustration was just as intense as their love. "Marriage is the first time that we're asked to love someone more than we love ourselves," the husband said. "This takes rearranging one's life in order to put the other person first. There will be things you don't like about your partner. There will be things that drive you completely nuts. It's not about changing your partner. It's about changing your perception of your partner and accepting her for who she is. Now that's love."

I heard it again and again. Now I simply pray that I can acquire that courage to love and accept someone for all that she is, just as she does for me. As for my perfect partner list? Let's just say it's fertilizing the grass.

Don't Blow Out the Candles

Dick and Molly Kohnstamm
Married 47 years

It's Halloween, 1961. Molly Kohnstamm's marriage is about to be forever changed by a very, very bad day.

This was a marriage still in its infancy, having begun two years earlier.

Molly met Dick at a job interview. At twenty-two and freshly graduated from the University of Minnesota, Molly applied for summer work at Timberline Lodge in Mount Hood, Oregon. Little did she know that she was applying for much more than waitressing work.

"I was asked to send my picture, my age . . . everything but my measurements before coming out," Molly remembers. "I think Dick might've chosen me as his 'summer girl' well before I got there. I was a goner, and I didn't even know it."

At the time, Dick was thirty-three and had been running Timberline for four years. When he took on the project in 1955, the formerly majestic mountain lodge had been all but given up on by the Forest Service, which owned it at the time. Due to poor management and years of neglect, the lodge that had been built by master craftsmen during the Great Depression had fallen into disrepair.

With no hotel or business experience, Dick decided he would change that. He spent years without taking a salary and paid skilled artisans to revitalize the interior and turn it into a luxury hotel with a beautiful, world-class dining room. He was in the process of turning Mount Hood into one of the nation's first off-season ski resorts. Due to Dick's detailed, long-term planning and ceaseless tenacity, the lodge was returning to its former glory. Dick used that same tenacious streak when it came to love. He immediately began pursuing Molly, flirting with her at every possible turn.

"I'm not interested in a romance," Molly told him.

"Fine," he replied. "We should just be friends, then. It's probably for the best."

"Right," Molly replied. "Definitely."

Two months later, Molly and Dick were engaged.

"He eventually just wore me down," Molly remembers. " 'Persistent' isn't really a strong enough word for Dick. I don't think they've come up with the word yet for him. Although those first couple years of marriage, I had a few choice ones."

When she married Dick, Molly didn't have any question in

her mind that he was the one. Though he was persistent and, some might even say, overbearing, something in her just knew that he would respect her and allow her to be who she was. And she was right. But after two years of marriage, she was wondering if that was enough.

"I'd discovered that we function at a very different pace, he and I," Molly says. "I think fast, I do things fast. He is much more measured and thinks things through."

Early on, Molly often mistook that thoughtfulness for Dick being slow, or simply not smart enough. She bristled at the time it took him to formulate a plan for even the simplest task. Should she ask him to change a lightbulb and wait for him to inspect the socket, consider the various wattages that might make sense? She began to worry that she was losing respect for him.

Additionally, Dick had dyslexia, a learning disability that makes it difficult to read and write, which only served to exacerbate the problem. Molly knew about his disability, but she had yet to fully understand all the ways it manifested itself.

Molly's concerns came to a head the day she gave birth to their first son, Kevin. Dick was sitting in the hospital room with her and the baby. They had recently moved to a house in Portland that didn't have a washer and dryer, so Molly asked him if he'd signed up for a diaper service as she'd asked him to do a few days earlier.

"No. I bought a washer and dryer at Meier and Frank," he replied. "There just aren't any diaper services in this town."

Molly had been in Portland for only a couple of months, but it was long enough to know that Meier and Frank was probably the most expensive department store in town.

"What? Honey, that's a terrible place to get appliances. They're completely overpriced," Molly barked, exhausted. "Besides, what do you mean there aren't any diaper services? I've seen their trucks driving around town, Dick. How is that possible?"

"Look, I've been through the yellow pages every possible way they could be listed, and they're just not here."

Molly shook her head in disbelief. This just couldn't be right. Then she had a thought. "Dick, how are you spelling 'diaper'?"

Dick responded confidently and without hesitation, "D-i-p-e-r."

Perhaps it was her raging hormones, but Molly wondered how she was going to raise a child with a man who couldn't do something as simple as spell "diaper."

Just a few months later, she would learn how.

It was Halloween day, and she and Dick were visiting her family in Anoka, Minnesota, the small town about twenty miles northwest of Minneapolis where Molly had grown up. The town's claim to fame? It had deemed itself the "Halloween Capital of the World" after hosting the first-ever Halloween parade in 1920. The parade began as a way to divert teenagers from Halloween pranks after citizens had dealt with one too many tipped-over outhouses and soaped windows the next morning. Later, Anoka could claim to be the hometown of Garrison Keillor, but in 1961, Halloween was pretty much its Big Thing.

That afternoon, Molly, Dick, her aunts, and her grandfather stood with the rest of the town along Main Street, waiting for the parade to start. There were children everywhere, in costumes, perched on the shoulders of their parents and in strollers. One woman in particular with a set of twins in a stroller caught Molly's eye—Molly had just learned she was pregnant with twins herself. She imagined the trials involved in having two children at once and hoped she and Dick would be up to the task.

The parade started, and the Halloween revelers began to pass by at the speed of Anoka—nice and slow, so everyone could get a good look. Little bears, ghosts, and witches walked past, waving furiously in homemade costumes as their parents proudly looked on. The local marching band, small as it was, gave its tuneful best. Police officers and firemen dressed as clowns adorned a fire truck and the entire Kiwanis Club sat uncomfortably on a hay bale float and grinned sheepishly as they waved to their wives.

But about a third of the way through the line, Molly noticed a car coming down the street that appeared to zigzag across both sides of the two-lane road. Its movements made Molly think it was a stunt car, but it wasn't decorated like any of the other vehicles in the parade.

"Well, that's just stupid," Molly thought. "You can't have a clown car pulling stunts like that so close to kids."

As the car came closer, Molly prepared herself to tell off that idiotic driver, but as it passed her, she realized that no one was behind the wheel. And as soon as that fact had registered, the car swerved one last time and, to her horror, barreled through the crowd of children on the other side of the street.

As she and Dick and the rest of her family ran across the street, the car finally came to a stop on the lawn of the local funeral parlor. The car door opened, and a man's slumped-over body fell out. Molly would later learn that he'd had a heart attack and died while driving. Surrounded by chaos, all she could do—all anyone seemed able to do—was stand there, devastated and stunned. But not Dick.

Molly looked around. "Where did Dick go?" she wondered. "He was standing next to me a moment ago."

She knew he'd been right next to her when the accident happened, so she wasn't concerned he was hurt, but she couldn't imagine where he'd gone. And then she saw him.

Dick emerged from the local armory with a large pile of blankets in his arms. He moved through the crowd of screaming people with the purpose and determination of a man who knew exactly what he was doing. All Molly could do was watch.

"I'd never seen anything like it," she recalls. "We were all just frozen with shock, but there was Dick in the middle of it, checking to see who needed the most help, calming people down, getting them the care they needed. He took control when no one else could. I watched him wrap a blanket around a crying boy and comfort his mother.

"And that was my 'aha!' moment. That was the moment when I realized that I'd misjudged this man. I thought, 'See, there's the difference. He stood, and he thought this through methodically, and then he accomplished what he set out to do.' "

After that day, things changed for Molly and Dick. Molly began to see Dick's strengths just as much as the things that drove her nuts and how their differences made them both better people.

That new way of thinking sustained Molly and Dick's marriage for forty-seven years, until Dick passed away in April of 2006 after a long illness. As Molly was taking care of Dick in his last years, she thought about all the years they'd had together, and

all that Dick had accomplished because of his tenacity and his un-
wavering ability to stick to a plan.

With his far-reaching goals, Dick turned Timberline into one
of the nation's first and best ski resorts. He pioneered the first
summer ski areas in the Northwest, becoming known as "the Father of Summer Skiing in America." And his legacy lives on
today, in the continued success of the resort his son now runs.
Molly claims that Timberline's waiting list is five years long, and
she attributes most of the success to Dick's fifty years of dedication to creating something extraordinary.

Seated in a comfortable den with walls adorned with awards,
tributes to Dick's professional legacy, Molly reflects on the importance of individuality in marriage. "Over time we learned to

let each other be ourselves. We accepted one another without interfering. And I believe it's because we were both independent that we were able to accomplish great things."

She smiles as she expresses her disdain for wedding ceremonies in which the bride and groom each use a candle to light a single candle, then blow their own out.

"You need to keep all those candles going," she urges. "Yes, use the two candles to light the other, but never blow out the other two. Keep your individuality, and never get into a relationship where someone tries to take away who you are. That's what loving my husband for forty-seven years taught me."

Fighting (Lovingly) to the Death

Wally and Cathy Moore
Married 50 years

In 1951, Wally Moore and Cathy Lakely were both freshman at Tufts University. The first time Cathy noticed Wally was in French class. Majoring in government, Cathy had to take French to fulfill her language requirement and sat in the back of the class each day, trying to call as little attention to herself as possible. Wally, on the other hand, was a French major, sitting at the front and feverishly raising his hand each time a question was posed. One day a fellow back-of-the-classer started to raise her hand to answer a question and Cathy admonished her.

"Don't raise your hand," she whispered, shaking her head. "That idiot up there is gonna answer all the questions anyway. Why bother?"

Ah. The beginning of a great romance.

Well, not exactly. Wally hadn't made the best impression with his know-it-all behavior. The two wouldn't cross paths again until senior year.

In April of that year, Cathy was living with her roommate Sharon in the Metcalf West dorm on campus, and Wally's fraternity brother Bill and Sharon happened to be dating. When the Mother's Day Dance rolled around, Sharon thought it would be much more fun to double-date, so she set up an evening with Wally and Cathy, who were in the school's theater group together by now. Cathy remembers that night like it was . . . well, a long time ago.

"He wasn't that interested in me, but he was fine with going on this double date," she recalls. "And we were both in theater together, so, it was . . . fine."

Ah. The beginning of a great romance.

Okay, not exactly then, either. Wally and Cathy continued to see each other in a strange are-we-dating-or-not limbo for a few weeks, going out to dinner and to see plays, but always going dutch, which annoyed Cathy. This was mostly because Wally didn't have a lot of money, but also because he couldn't quite figure out how he felt about Cathy. That is, until another man helped him gain some clarity.

Wally and Cathy had been working together on a production of *A Connecticut Yankee in King Arthur's Court.* Wally, who was now studying design, was the costumer. Cathy, who had been in theatrical productions since she was ten, was playing Morgan Le Fay, a sultry femme fatale and the female lead.

"She couldn't sing a note," Wally recalls now, smiling.

"No, I couldn't," Cathy concurs slyly, striking a coquettish pose. "The director cast me because he thought I could *move.*"

Apparently there were some other boys who thought so, too. On the last night of the play, during intermission, Wally brought up the subject of a night on the town.

"I can't," Cathy said. "I have a date."

"Oh. Well. Great," Wally replied, his face flushed with anger.

Wally sat through the rest of the play in silence. After the curtain call, he made a beeline for Metcalf West. Ignoring the "Welcome Home, Cathy and Wally!" sign that had been put up at the building's entrance to celebrate the last night of the play, he went inside to confront Cathy.

"What the hell was that?" he yelled in the building's lobby.

"I'm sorry. You should've told me you wanted to go out after the show," Cathy responded calmly. "And I guess I don't understand. Are we exclusive?"

Wally waffled, as usual, which drove her crazy. He knew he had feelings for her, his jealousy was proof of that, but his hardheadedness just wouldn't let him fully admit it. It took a tragedy to do that.

After graduation, Cathy planned to go to Washington, D.C.,

to work as a secretary for the CIA. Wally was planning to attend the Yale School of Drama for set design. Though they had feelings for each other, they thought it was best to go their separate ways. That Sunday, Father's Day, Cathy got on a bus headed for her home twenty miles north of Boston. As the bus drove into town, Cathy had a sense that something was wrong. From the bus station, she ran to her nearby home, only to find her worst fear realized: Her father had died of a massive heart attack.

Wally found out through a mutual friend and showed up the afternoon of Cathy's father's funeral, chocolate cake in hand.

"Chocolate cake?" Cathy remembers, smiling. "It was so odd of him to do that. But very sweet. Anyway, I guess we found out during that time that we had a lot more in common than we thought we did."

Cathy and Wally spent the next few days talking and discovered that their friendship and romance had grown much deeper. So much so that Cathy decided to forgo her move to D.C. to live closer to Wally. Two years later, they were married.

Throughout the ensuing fifty years of marriage, their mutual hardheadedness and tendency toward friendly bickering remained. In fact, Wally taught the formerly soft-spoken Cathy to yell like a champ (well, he either "taught her" or "drove her to it," one or the other). And through raising three children, multiple job changes, and moves, they managed to keep things together. For most of that time, Wally worked various jobs and even owned a business, and Cathy was the "CEO of the house." That is, until they moved to Colorado and Cathy became a highly successful real estate agent.

"That's when I told him that he'd supported the family for

forty years, now it was time I supported him," Cathy says. "That was when *he* became CEO of the house."

And with the shift in roles came fun new things to bicker about. Like the dishwasher.

"For ten years, I've kept house," Wally asserts. "I'm very organized, and I've developed a certain way of putting dishes in the dishwasher. So when she puts hers in, I rearrange them."

"The way he does it, it looks good, but the water doesn't get on them enough," Cathy retorts.

"I tell her she should just walk away from it—"

"I can't walk away from it, because it's annoying."

"It's annoying because you still want some authority in the kitchen," Wally says finally. "But it's my domain now."

Cathy rolls her eyes and acquiesces. This time.

Their most recent issue with driving each other nuts is a doozy, though. It's about their burial plots.

Wally grew up on the East Coast in a large family, in which visiting the graves of family members was a Memorial Day tradition. His cousins, aunts, and uncles would come into town, his mother would make flower baskets, and they'd make the rounds. Then they'd go out to a special dinner where they'd toast the memory of lost loved ones. So it was very important to Wally that he and Cathy have grave sites that were easy for their children to visit. He chose a plot in a cemetery that was convenient for them.

Cathy, however, had already chosen a Catholic cemetery that was a lot less accessible. Their daughter, Buffy, visited the plot Wally had chosen and told Cathy she wouldn't want to be buried there, as it was too close to a train track and the view wasn't very good. A good view was important to Cathy.

"I didn't understand why a view would be important if you were in the ground," Wally says.

"I'd like to be buried someplace beautiful," Cathy responds.

She was also put off by the fact that Wally had simply made the decision without considering her feelings. They fought about it for a couple of weeks. And then Cathy let it go. She realized that this one thing was much more important to Wally than it was to her, and that fighting to the death about it would get them nowhere—except to the plot!

For Wally and Cathy, this was the lesson they felt they had to teach. Fighting is inevitable, but it should never be about winning. It should be about finding the best solution to a problem and knowing when it's time to let go. Knowing that, at times, giving in means giving your partner something that truly means something to him or her.

"Nothing is easy in this world that's worth something," says Wally. "And sometimes it's hard to come to a compromise. It helps to recognize that when it's a big deal to the other person, let them have it, and know there is a trade-off coming."

"Plus, I've learned to accept and let go of the little things," Cathy says.

Wally shoots her a look. "Oh . . . like the dishwasher?"

Cathy ignores Wally and smiles. "You can't change people. In life you have two choices: You can be right or you can be happy."

Of course, neither of the Moores was too happy when, after finally making a decision, they discovered the price of the plot had gone up by fifty percent, which gave them something new to fight about. But all that counts is that in the end, they'll be together. Just hope you don't get a plot nearby, because they'll probably bicker their way through eternity.

Learn Your Lesson, Then Teach It

Ruth and Eddie Elcott
Married 63 years

September 1942, downtown Chicago. Eddie Elcott, an army private, was in his element. Having just arrived in the Windy City for radio training, he learned of a USO/Jewish Welfare Board–sponsored dance where Jewish soldiers could have a home-cooked meal and cut a rug with some nice girls. The meal sounded great, but it was the dancing that sold Eddie.

Growing up, Eddie's playground was the streets of Harlem in New York City. His family struggled through the Great Depression, his father a tradesman in leather goods, his mother a seamstress. When he wasn't in the public library reading everything he could get his hands on, Eddie was learning to do what it seemed everyone else in his neighborhood could already do: dance.

That night at the USO party, Eddie ruled the floor. Girls were practically lined up to dance with him, pouting coyly, "Eddie! Why haven't you danced with me yet?" Eventually, he'd get to

just about all of them. Except one. As he danced, he spotted a girl with sparkling eyes at a table just beyond the piano player. He couldn't take his eyes off her. It was Ruth Meyer.

Ruth came from a wealthy and very traditional Jewish family in Germany. Until she was seventeen years old, her life was idyllic—her mother never had to work, and because her family always had maids, neither did Ruth. But when the Nazis came into power, everything changed. Ruth was forced to escape Germany with everything she owned in eleven suitcases to work as a housemaid on a farm in England. It was from there that she managed, through sheer tenacity, to convince the English consulate to help get her mother, father, and sister out of Germany. She succeeded in doing so just three days before the start of World War II. But many of her family members—including her grandparents and her only cousin—weren't so lucky. After that, her family wanted to get as far away as possible and moved to Chicago to begin again.

So having lived through her own trials, Ruth was just as savvy as Eddie in her own way. And she had his number.

"He was constantly staring at me over the shoulders of other girls," Ruth remembers. "I thought, 'What a wolf. I can't stand that guy.'"

And like a cat that's inexplicably drawn to the only allergic person in the room, Eddie left the gaggle of girls that had surrounded him all night and approached Ruth.

"Would you like to dance?" he asked casually.

"I don't think so," she responded. "Not with you."

"Oh. Well, y'know, I'm tired anyway," Eddie said, moving

toward the empty seat next to Ruth. "Do you mind if we just sit here and talk?"

Ruth apprehensively agreed. And somehow that night, Eddie managed to charm Ruth just enough to get invited to Shabbat dinner the following week.

Shabbat is the traditional day of rest in Judaism, beginning before sundown on Friday and ending after nightfall on Saturday. On Friday night, the woman of the house recites the kiddush, or Shabbat blessing, and lights two candles. Ruth was still living with her parents, so her mother, always a powerful matriach, recited the prayer and they all sat down to eat: Eddie, Ruth, her parents, her sister . . . and Freddy, Ruth's ex-boyfriend. Ruth had just had a painful breakup with Freddy, but he'd already been invited to Shabbat so they had to honor the invitation. This was something Eddie hadn't counted on, but he took it in stride. Eddie sat next to Ruth and Freddy sat at the other end of the table near Ruth's father.

Even with the odd guest list, it was turning out to be a lovely Shabbat. Ruth had been concerned about Eddie's rough upbringing, but he was clearly smart and definitely witty, and her mother seemed to approve. That is, until Eddie had an itch on his head and scratched it . . . with his *fork*. Ruth looked on in horror, as if it were happening in slow motion. She saw her mother's eyes widen and her sister break into a surprised grin. Thankfully, Ruth's father was too nearsighted to catch it, but still she thought this was the end of Eddie. Strangely, though, the dinner simply went on as if nothing had happened.

At the end of the night, the changing of the boyfriend guard had occurred, and Ruth and Eddie began dating in earnest. Eddie continued his army training and spent every free moment with Ruth. They went to movies, danced many a night away, and spent quite a few dinners with Ruth's family, where Eddie used his fork only in the manner in which it was intended. After six months, Eddie finished his training in Chicago and received orders to return to California. Ruth was devastated but promised to write him letters. Eddie told her that he wasn't the greatest correspondent, but he'd try.

For five months Ruth and Eddie wrote letters, with Eddie, more of a reader than a writer, working hard to hold up his end of the bargain. At the end of those five months, Eddie received word from the army that he was shipping out to New Guinea in a month. And that's when he wrote the Big One. Eddie proposed to Ruth in a letter.

Ruth begged her parents to let her go to California to marry Eddie before he shipped out. "He's shipping out in a month," she told them.

Ruth got on a train to California the next day. As soon as she arrived, she and Eddie found themselves a "rolling rabbi," grabbed two witnesses, and got hitched. Then they had a beautiful three-week honeymoon in sunny California, which Ruth fell in love with at the same time she was falling deeper in love with Eddie. At the end of three weeks, they said a tearful good-bye.

Ruth returned to Chicago only to discover that she was pregnant. Eight months later, Ruth had Diane, their first daughter. As she received daily updates from Eddie on his activities, Ruth sent daily updates on Diane. First solid food, first crawl, first steps.

Eddie met his daughter through pictures and words, and that's how she met her dad. It was almost two years before Eddie's first tour was over, and when Diane was eighteen months old, her father finally came home.

Ruth had rented a tiny one-bedroom apartment in appalling condition and fixed it up as much as she could.

The evening he came home, they stayed up all night talking on the couch, with baby Diane at Ruth's parents' house so they could have privacy. Even though they knew almost every detail of each other's lives for the past two years, they couldn't help feeling a little like strangers. And, as it turned out, readjusting to life together was a struggle.

When Ruth's parents brought Diane back to the apartment, Ruth immediately took her to Eddie, saying, "This is your daddy!"

Diane looked confused. She went into her nursery to get Eddie's picture.

"No," she cried. "This is my daddy."

And Diane wasn't the only woman in the house Eddie was having trouble with.

A few weeks after Eddie arrived home, it was Mother's Day. Ruth awaited the day with great anticipation—her first Mother's Day with her husband. Growing up, Mother's Day, like all holidays, had been a huge deal. Her mother would stay in bed, and the family would bring her a gift and at least one of her favorite flower, calla lily, which was very rare in Germany at the time. She couldn't wait to see what Eddie had in store for her, especially since he'd missed her first two Mother's Days while he was overseas.

She woke up that morning and took a look around the room. No flowers yet. Eddie slept. No breakfast in bed. She got up to feed Diane and started breakfast.

"Hmph. Must be coming later," she thought.

It wasn't. As the day progressed, she realized that Eddie had nothing planned for her. No gifts, no flowers, not even a "Happy Mother's Day." She was incensed. A year and a half of raising their daughter without him, and he doesn't even remember Mother's Day?

Late in the afternoon, a small argument started, probably over something petty like garbage day or who ate the last pickle, but it exploded into something much more serious. Suddenly, Ruth was crying.

"...and...and...you didn't even remember it was Mother's Day!" she screamed. "How could you forget, after everything I've done?"

"What? Wait a minute." Eddie was completely thrown.

"What kind of a person does that?" Ruth continued her rant. "What kind of person forgets his own wife, the mother of his child, on their first Mother's Day together!? I...I...just... can't..."

Ruth ran to the bathroom, sobbing and trying to pull off her wedding ring. She finally got it off, threw it into the toilet, and reached for the chain. But she couldn't pull it.

Eddie was immediately at her side, apologizing over and over again as he fished her ring out of the bowl. He didn't have an excuse for her, but he had a simple explanation: He just didn't know.

Eddie had grown up without holidays, or at least without holidays that looked anything like Ruth's. There were no toys on Hanukkah, perhaps a small celebration on birthdays, but certainly no recognition of Mother's Day. Eddie had learned what a family looked like from his own parents, but they weren't concerned with remembering holidays, or even with taking the time to teach Eddie what it was like to be a father and a husband. So Eddie did have a learning curve, but he was an eager pupil. And Ruth was happy to teach him.

As they ran into issues, they talked them out, sometimes all through the night. Some fights turned into discussions, some discussions into fights, but the roller coaster always ended up in the same place: with them together, and with a better understanding of each other.

Eddie learned to love buying gifts, and sometimes for no reason.

"We would pass a jewelry store," Ruth remembers, "and Eddie would say, 'Let's go in and get you something.' I'd say that it wasn't my birthday, but it didn't matter. He wanted to buy me something. And who am I to argue?"

Ruth and Eddie raised three children, joyfully celebrating every holiday of their sixty-three years together. And they've passed their love of celebrations on to their children and grandchildren. One anniversary, the whole family, children and grandchildren, dressed in Oriental garb for a Chinese-theme party complete with mini-gazebos. One Passover, their son David put up tents in the living room and had them re-enact the exodus from Egypt. And one Hanukkah, Diane gave each member of the family a sculpture of Ruth's mother, whom they called Mútti, holding a single piece of a crystal bowl that had survived the run from the Nazis but not a California earthquake.

And on the Sabbath, Ruth and Eddie's grandchildren and great-grandchildren gather around Mútti's statue and sing her a special song, just for the mother of the house, the song Ruth used to sing to her. And as Eddie watches, he knows that he may not have learned what it meant to be a father from his parents, but because he was open and willing to admit his mistakes, he did learn.

"Wisdom is different from intelligence," Eddie says. "It's based on experience. You learn by living. And with the right amount of commitment, you can live through any issue."

Ruth and Eddie still have the letters they wrote to each other during the war—more than two thousand of them. A couple of years ago, their family convinced them to pull them out again. Eddie didn't think they could've survived sixty-three years in an old leather suitcase (one of the very suitcases Ruth took on her trip out of Germany). Moving from garages to basements to attics, he thought they must be ruined. But when he opened the latch, there they were, completely intact.

They numbered them to make sure they stayed in order, and they started reading them to each other. Some weeks, it's letters every night, sometimes every couple of weeks, but each letter they read reminds them of how much they loved each other then and how much they still love each other now.

Many letters contain information all but completely erased from their memory. Ruth will read a particularly passionate passage from Eddie and blush. Eddie will read one of Ruth's detailed letters about Diane's first year and be reminded of his young wife's dedication to making sure he didn't miss anything while he was away. Beautiful surprises in every envelope.

Today, seated together on their living room couch with not an inch separating their bodies, they look upon their love letters stacked high in antique boxes with admiration, recognizing the vast amount of effort it has taken for them to gain an understanding of one another despite their many differences.

"*Try* to understand," Ruth emphasizes. "You'll never *fully* understand your mate. That's basic, that's genetic."

Eddie makes a cue that he needs the floor. "One key to getting through the irritations," he winds up, "is to try and play the role of the other person. Mentally stand in their shoes for a while. More often than not you'll see you weren't so right after all. Also, pick your battles. Keep things in proper perspective. Ask yourself: If my wife were gone, would I really care about this? You'll find that in this frame of mind, most things are petty.

"And so we developed a motto, you see," he continues. "We generally say, 'Divorce—' "

"That's me, I'm saying that!" Ruth cuts in.

"All right, all right," Eddie concedes, leaning in to touch his forehead to hers.

"We said this many times, when people ask the question, 'Did you ever think about divorce?' The answer I usually give them is—and I mean it—divorce? Seldom, if ever. Murder? Often!"

Chapter 3

What's Missing from Today's Marriages?

KID OBLIVIOUS

—by Jason

Now fourteen years later, the morning Mat announced his parents' breakup is a memory still etched vividly in my mind. I have yet to see someone's character shift so dramatically. I have yet to see eyes so full of hurt.

The moment he stepped on the school bus I knew something was wrong. Everything about him seemed off. Usually the effervescent comedian in our group of junior high buddies, he sat down next to me without saying a word, hoodie pulled low over his face.

After miles of awkward silence, I asked him what was up. No answer. I shrugged it off and asked again.

"My parents broke up," he muttered without looking up.

"Your parents?" Impossible. I knew his parents were fine. "Are you joking?"

No response.

"I don't get it," I said. "What do you mean they broke up?"

"They're getting a divorce," he spat. "How else do you want me to f***ing put it?"

I was stunned. He never swore like that, especially not at me, his best buddy. And those eyes—weepy and bloodshot, loaded with disgust, fierce—they made him look ten years older. His stable, loving home was gone. Life as he knew it was gone. And he seemed fully willing to beat my ass to the ground just in case I *really* wanted to know how bad this stuff felt.

My friends knew me as Kid Oblivious. Divorce was a totally foreign concept to me. In fact, marital strife was a foreign concept to me. While some of my friends had to deal with drunken, high, sometimes even suicidal parents who cussed each other out every other night and threw plates at each other on the nights in between, I grew up in a simple, sheltered world. My dad was home for dinner at 6 P.M. sharp. He'd share a loving salutation with my mom, maybe a little peck on the lips. Mom would have a home-cooked meal ready to go on the table, glasses full of cold one percent milk, tossed salad. My brothers and sisters and I would sit at the table and discuss the day's adventures. I'd try to eat more casserole than Dad.

Naïveté neatly forged my glossy expectations around marriage. Once I found my special somebody, a woman I loved and who loved me, I'd be cool. Sure, we'd likely disagree over silly stuff like asparagus versus peas or red paint versus green, but I knew those issues would disappear once we'd sharpened up our effective communication skills (at the snap of our fingers perhaps?). We'd have asparagus one night, peas the next; her side of the bedroom could be painted red, mine green—problems solved. I was certain that marital longevity would take care of itself.

So when the Marriage Masters over and over explained that the main virtue missing from today's marriages was commitment, my tendency was to slough it off: *Are they trying to suggest marriage is difficult? That marriage takes work?*

And how, Kid Oblivious, and how.

Statistics say that most marriages that fail do so within eight years. It's safe to say I wouldn't have lasted eight months with my expectations. Let there be no confusion: Behind every successful, lifelong marriage is a massive amount of hard work and difficult moments, when each spouse wanted out but instead reconfirmed a resolution to stick to it, for better or worse. ("Stick-to-itiveness" was a word our interviewees used often.)

This isn't to say that the Marriage Masters simply swept their garbage under the rug and lived forty-plus years in quiet misery. On the contrary, their definition of commitment meant getting through the trouble spots to rediscover what had made them happy together in the first place. It meant apologies. It meant forgiveness. It meant humility. It meant dedication and rededication a hundred times over. If the relationship reached a boiling point, *something* had to change—only the marital status could not be one of those *somethings*. As one Marriage Master said, "Marriage is the toughest job you will ever do in your life."

Many Marriage Masters recounted extreme circumstances they'd survived together: bankruptcies, depressions, severe hospitalizations, natural disasters, or near-fatal accidents. Several couples broke down into tears as they relived their trials of losing a son or daughter. Needless to say, these circumstances rip apart even the strongest couples. But deep and mutual commitment—plus an unshakable belief that marriage is a bed of roses, thorns included—was a consistent theme in these Marriage Masters' survival stories.

But it isn't just acts of God that can threaten commitment. Internal struggles, the buildup of resentment and bruised faith, can have the same effect.

Bob and Lorolei Brown made this clear to me when describing their first twenty-five years of marriage in their Oregon farmhouse.

Recalling the moment their love story began, Lorolei said, "I was drinking coffee at the diner Bob worked at, and a little old blind man came in and ordered milk toast. His waitress slapped a piece of toast and a glass of cold milk on the table. The man felt around for it and after finding it said, 'No, ma'am, I'd like it in a bowl and warm the milk please.' The waitress huffed and puffed and grabbed it, smooshed the toast in a bowl, then poured the cold milk over it and brought it back.

"Well, Bob saw what was going on and came over to the blind man and asked him what he wanted. The man told him and Bob said, 'I know exactly what you want.' He made some new toast, cut it up into a bowl, warmed up the milk, and brought it back to the man.

"I fell in love immediately," she says. "Wholly in love."

Twenty-four years into their marriage, being "wholly in love" with Bob seemed unfathomable to Lorolei. Like many husbands, Bob entered matrimony with the mentality that making a living was the best way to show how much he loved his wife and kids. Before long, making a living was the *only* way he was showing love. Gone from 6 A.M. to 9 P.M. managing a restaurant, he returned home with no energy to spare. He never made it to his children's awards ceremonies, parent-teacher conferences, sporting events, or family dinners. He seldom touched his wife, let alone talked with her.

At this point, Bob looked down at the buttons on his shirt, sheepish, while Lorolei recounted her boiling point.

"When I said my wedding vows," she said to Mat and me

with a firm look, "I said them with every ounce of conviction in my heart. I took those vows *very, very* seriously. But after twenty-some years of not having a husband or a father for our kids, I'd had enough.

"One night, I finally lost it. I looked at our son and daughter across the dinner table, nearly all grown up. Bob, of course wasn't there. And I was overwhelmed with the realization that my kids' dad had seen none of their upbringing. So I threw the plates in the sink and stormed outside into the field. And I screamed up to the stars at the top of my lungs, 'Lord, I know I promised you till death do us part, so either you take him or you take me because this is not working anymore!' "

"Fortunately," Bob said with a grim smile, "that was one of those times when the Lord did it his way rather than hers."

"But to say that our marriage wasn't good would be an egregious understatement," he continued. "We really didn't like each other at that point. I was so sure that my rationale for neglecting the relationship was solid, that I was the one making the living so I shouldn't have to work as hard on the relationship."

"Our marriage felt hopeless," Lorolei said.

The deeper the Browns got into their story of marital dissatisfaction, the more uncomfortable I became. I was reminded of all the conversations I'd had with friends about their parents' divorces, and how—as was the case with the Browns' crisis—the root causes always seemed so inextricably complex—too complex for anybody, including the marriage counselors from whom they'd sought help, to resolve. These problems weren't the asparagus vs. peas marital hiccups that I'd felt so prepared to overcome; these problems went deep, lying buried under layer upon layer of mistakes and misunderstandings, perpetuated by years, sometimes decades, of ignorance or pride or denial, or even shame. Quagmires like theirs didn't have solutions on speed dial.

This reality hit me hard because when I was faced with relationship conflicts that didn't seem to have a quick and easy solution, I'd always relied on one fix-all: I ran. Ran quickly. Didn't look back. Didn't answer questions. I'd just shrugged my shoulders, tossed off some self-deprecatory "but it's never been a secret that I'm a commitmentphobe" garbage, reasoned with myself that it was okay to bail "because it's not like we were married," and kept running, back to the less-complicated world of singledom.

I liked to think that I'd be able to turn that mentality and behavior around whenever I got married, that I'd choose to *fight for* my marriage rather than *flight from* my marriage, but . . . will I? Turning Bob and Lorolei's story over in my head, I had to question myself: *How am I going to survive this stuff when I get married?*

"The important thing in times like that," Lorolei emphasized, "is to remind yourself why you married this person in the first place."

"That's right," Bob agreed. "I thought to myself, 'There's a reason why I fawned all over this woman in the beginning and there's a reason why I thought she was the most important person in the world.' I decided to put myself back in that mode."

"Which I didn't respond to at all," Lorolei said.

"She was suspicious," Bob said, "which is the biggest obstacle to resuscitating a marriage after that many years of neglect—to recapture that faith we once had in the relationship. It took a lot of humility and a lot of patience—"

"And a lot of long drives with me in the car," Lorolei said.

"And on our twenty-fifth anniversary," Bob continued, "we met our goal of renewing our vows, which was very symbolic for me. I don't know if men ever fully understand the word 'commitment,' but I sure learned a lot about it that year."

"I don't understand," Mat said. "What did you change, Bob? Your job?"

"My attitude," Bob replied. "On the outside you wouldn't have seen massive changes other than me paying more attention to her."

"Yes, boys," Lorolie said to us with a warm smile, "women do tend to enjoy that."

"But the most important changes were probably on the inside," Bob continued. "I tried to look at her as I had while courting her. I made it a point to prove and re-prove to her that she is the most important person in my life and every day was a new opportunity to win 'us' back."

Lorolei gave Bob a proud look and squeezed his hand tightly. "He's doing it right now," she said, leaning into her husband of forty-three years for a compassionate kiss.

Marriage Masters like the Browns have given my future marriage a supreme gift with this lesson on commitment: On the other side of an "unsolvable marital crisis" is a path that returns to love. It's not going to be an obvious path, but it's there. It's not going to be an easy path, but a steadfast decision to work through it will pay off. And when I do hit the rough patches of marriage, I'm going to think back to the way Bob and Lorolei Brown and so many other Marriage Masters held hands with such an impressive reverence for each other, their love stronger than ever. If the Marriage Masters can do it, then so can I. The rewards will be worth every ounce of effort.

Wait, hold on—did I just use the word "effort"? Did I finally acknowledge that marriage is difficult? Indeed I did.

After Bob and Lorolei, the lesson in the marital reality of commitment came full circle when I recently interviewed my parents. I asked them why, in twenty-eight years, I'd never seen them fight.

"Because you weren't born yet. I told him we were finished within the first month," my mom answered. "I had no idea marriage would be that hard!"

"Aha!" I thought. "So that's where I got it from."

"I told her divorce was not a word in our vocabulary," my dad added.

And finally, Kid Oblivious gets it.

You Gotta Have Faith . . .

Jim and Marie Hooten
Married 54 years

"I want my husband back!" Marie Hooten wrote, her spiky black handwriting messier than usual in her rush to get the

words she had been thinking for over a year finally down on paper. "The man I married is gone—he's absent from everything, and I want him back."

She sealed the letter in an envelope, then hesitated, looking over at the bed where Jim, her husband of thirty-four years, lay sleeping off his latest bender. Marie had never had the courage to tell Jim how she felt about his drinking. But on that winter night in 1984, she had finally reached her limit. As much as she loved her husband, she couldn't go on living the life they had together.

Over the past year, Jim's drinking had progressed from a couple of beers on a Saturday night to an all-consuming addiction. Alcohol had replaced friends, replaced family, even, as Jim later recalled with a wry smile, replaced God as the thing he cared for and worshipped most.

Marie knew that if their marriage had any hope of surviving, Jim needed to get his drinking under control. She also knew that unless she did something drastic, he wouldn't seek help on his own. So she poured her anger and frustration and sorrow into a letter, and lay it in the bureau drawer where Jim would see it the next morning when he was sober enough to get ready for work. Then she did the only thing she could think of to save her marriage—she turned and walked out of it.

Marie had never imagined that her life would take such a dramatic turn, especially after so many years together.

The couple met in 1951, at the end of Marie's senior year of high school. After a whirlwind courtship, they were married six weeks later. And for many years they were happy. Jim was a successful salesman and quickly rose through the ranks at his company, but he still made Marie and their four children a priority. Jim coached his sons' baseball teams; Jim and Marie went dancing on weekends, were active members of their church, and had a busy social calendar.

At first, they both would have a couple of drinks when they went out for the night. They'd meet friends for steak dinners at the Elks Club or gambling at the American Legion Club, and enjoy a beer or cocktail as part of the fun. But alcohol gradually began to play a bigger and bigger part in their nights out, until eventually, their entire social life revolved around it.

Jim realized he was having a problem, but he tried to hide it from his friends. As his alcoholism grew worse, those nights out with Marie grew less and less frequent. Jim's disease had progressed to the point where his liver could no longer metabolize alcohol, so it took only a couple of drinks to make Jim completely drunk. He didn't want to be around anybody, because he was worried about embarrassing himself, but he still wanted to drink. He just preferred to do it at home, where he could quietly get plastered and be in bed by 7:30, without risking making a fool of himself in public.

Marie began turning down invitations from friends, because she knew that all Jim wanted to do was hibernate. She missed the dancing and companionship and fun but continued to put off the friends. Jim made it clear that he didn't want people to see him. And while Marie wanted her social life back, she didn't want to do anything to humiliate her husband.

Eventually, the invitations became less frequent, until one day they stopped altogether. Marie looked around at her life and realized that she was completely alone. She'd put off her old friends so many times that they had simply faded away, her children were grown and out of the house, and Jim had checked out, emotionally, mentally, and spiritually.

Marie knew that her marriage was in serious trouble, but she wasn't aware of how much damage Jim's drinking was actually causing. Part of the problem was that, at the time, neither of them realized exactly what alcoholism was.

Jim's sales route took him through Skid Row. He would step over drunks sleeping in doorways and think that *that* was what alcoholics were. Surely those pitiful, broken men had nothing in common with Jim, who never missed a day's work, never got a traffic ticket, and was, for all appearances, a solid, upstanding family man.

Marie also didn't realize that Jim's drinking was more than just a problem—it was an actual illness. She had grown up with a high-functioning alcoholic father who, much like Jim, managed to keep his addiction hidden behind closed doors. She wasn't aware of the signs of alcoholism; to her, life with Jim was no different from life with her dad.

And that wasn't where the similarity ended. As a little girl, Marie had been taught that her father had the final word in family discussions—what he said went. Marie went into marriage deferring to Jim. His word was law when it came to decisions—Marie didn't have a say in how their marriage was run . . . until the December evening when she summoned the courage to write Jim that letter.

I want my husband back!

With those five words, Marie had finally found her voice.

Two days before Christmas in 1984, Jim Hooten woke up with a pounding headache, a queasy stomach, and the knowledge that if he didn't make some changes, life as he knew it would be over.

Jim had always prided himself on his ability to maintain the appearance of control—a good job, a loving wife, a beautiful home—even when inside he felt wildly out of control. But reading Marie's letter was a wake-up call. For the first time ever, he was aware that he was slipping. Sales at work were slipping, and now his marriage was slipping. And the only way to keep his life from slipping away was to quit drinking.

Marie spent two weeks away, visiting their eldest son in Mexico, and Jim got a glimpse of what life would be like without her. It was a grim picture, and Jim knew that if he wanted to fix his marriage, he had to fix himself. It was a new year, so he made a private resolution to stop drinking.

But alcohol turned out to be too big an addiction to beat on his own. Two weeks after Marie returned home, the couple went to their daughter's house for a Super Bowl party. Jim brought along a case of beer, ostensibly as a gift for his son-in-law. He ended up drinking most of the case himself. When they went home that evening, an already-drunk Jim chased the beer with a few glasses of brandy. He went to take a shower, and as he stood there, the pounding water matching the pounding in his head, he had a revelation: He couldn't do it alone.

He'd tried to stop drinking by himself and had already failed. Jim had needed Marie's leaving to get him to face his problem; now he needed her support if he was going to overcome it.

He got out of the shower, put on his best suit and tie, and went out to the living room, where Marie was sitting. Jim looked at her and started crying.

"I need help."

Marie also had tears in her eyes as she got up from the couch and put her arms around her husband. Since she'd been back from Mexico, Jim hadn't mentioned the letter to her, had refused to admit he'd read it at all, but as she looked at her husband weeping and asking for her help, she knew that he'd gotten her message loud and clear.

Jim jokes that for him, alcohol had taken the place of God, but Marie had never lost faith. Her whole life, whenever she encountered a problem too big to handle alone, she asked God for help. She wrote the letter to Jim as a way of asking God what to do about Jim, and, "as usual," she says with a chuckle, "God had a good answer."

That night, Jim checked into a residential treatment program for alcoholism. As he started his journey to become sober, he refound his faith—in God, in the twelve steps, in his wife, and, most of all, in himself. Jim spent thirty-one days in rehab to overcome his addiction.

Marie spent the time Jim was away working in a program of her own—Al-Anon. She learned about the disease and ways to support Jim in his recovery. She learned that she was not alone. But most important, she learned that she *did* have a voice in their relationship. It was the strength of that voice that had prompted her to write the letter, and it was because of that voice that she got what she wished for: her husband back.

After Jim returned from the treatment facility, the couple's life changed again, this time for the better. While they lost the few remaining friends they had whose lives revolved around drinking with them, they started to build new relationships.

They found ways to go out and be social that didn't involve alcohol. They began to explore a new dynamic to their marriage, where they both can have a say, and their voices can both be heard. And above all else, they rediscovered their love for and commitment to each other. They realized that they could handle any hurdle, no matter how great, as long as they were together.

It's been twenty years since Jim stood in his living room and asked his wife for help, and he has not had a drink since. His continued sobriety inspired their three sons, who were all battling addictions of their own, to seek treatment, and today, all four Hooten men are clean and sober.

Looking back on the snowy night when she wrote Jim the letter that changed their lives, Marie has no regrets. Her faith in and commitment to her husband got them through one difficult year of a fifty-four-year marriage. And while there are still the occasional bumps in the road, that's just part of what commitment is really about.

"Every day you've got to work on your marriage," she says with a shrug, her hand resting comfortably in Jim's. "Some days are better than others. You know, in marriage everyone expects the better, the richer, and the health. When you say your vows, recognize that there will come a day when God calls on you to walk through the worse, the poorer, and the sickness."

"But like the program says," Jim adds, looking at Marie with a smile, "all you can do is take it one day at a time . . . and never give up."

> ### *The Great Depression*
>
> **Dale and Corrine Goldsmith**
> **Married 50 years**

Dale Goldsmith slowly hung up the phone as his wife, Corrine, walked into the living room.

"Steve Gusick is dead. He killed himself," Dale said.

"Oh my God. That's terrible. Why would he do something like that?" Corrine asked.

"It's the recession," Dale said. "He lost all his money, all their rental properties. He had no commissions coming in. There was talk that Steve thought his wife might leave, just like Art's wife left a few months ago. So he sat down at the kitchen table, wrote his wife a note, and put a bullet through his head."

Steve had been employed by the real estate company in Newberg where Dale worked as a manager. Art headed the company, which had about thirty-five offices and several hundred employees spread out all over the area. Everyone loved his job, loved the bosses and, until the recession hit, they'd all made good money.

Dale didn't know what to think anymore. If this could happen to Steve—who seemed to be such a handsome, charismatic, ambitious young man—could anybody really be safe? Little by little, all his hopes and plans and even the family's security seemed to be slipping away.

As if she were reading her husband's mind, Corrine reassured Dale, "Don't you worry. We'll get through this."

Dale smiled at his wife. He was the one everyone always called the incurable optimist. Now here she was reminding him.

"There's got to be a way," Dale thought. He decided to redouble his efforts and follow every lead, no matter how slim, until he turned things around for his family.

Over the next few months, Dale worked as hard as he knew how. But something was missing. The work held no joy for him anymore, and not just because people had started tightening their belts and stopped buying real estate. He couldn't muster up his old passion. At first he thought that Steve's suicide had hit him particularly hard. But after a while, he had to acknowledge that something else was also going on.

Dale was depressed.

For a while he tried to hide it and pretend that everything was normal. But when the depression started affecting his relationship with Corrine, they decided to see a doctor. The specialist told them that Dale suffered from intimacy issues related to low testosterone levels.

"The cause could be any one of several things," the doctor said. "All we really know is that for some reason you've just stopped making testosterone. But that's okay. We can give you shots."

"What about the other symptoms?" Dale asked. "The fatigue and the—"

"You just come in every month," the doctor assured him. "We'll give you a shot and you'll be fine."

Dale and Corrine thanked the doctor and left.

"It's going to be okay," Corrine said on the way to the car. "You know that, don't you?"

Dale squeezed his wife's hand and half smiled. They'd come through worse than this before. He had to believe that they'd be all right this time too.

So once a month for the next few years, Dale dutifully showed up at the doctor's office to get a shot. While the testosterone injections did help improve their sex life, they did nothing to ease the sadness and lethargy that had slowly overtaken him. Dale, who was always so full of vibrancy and life, could now barely get out of bed some mornings.

By the early eighties, the worst of the recession had passed and things started looking up.

Unfortunately, Art's business hadn't made it that far. Though the loss devastated him, Dale still got out there and scrambled to get a job with another agency. When he found one, he and Corrine figured things would get better. But Dale just didn't have his old fire anymore. The worst part was that none of the doctors they'd been to could help him figure out what was wrong.

Corrine knew what her husband was going through. For years, she'd suffered with debilitating bouts of fatigue. And, just like with Dale, doctor after doctor told her that it was all in her head. Though chronic fatigue syndrome wouldn't be recognized for many years, she'd suffered through the pain and frustration of not being listened to or taken seriously. Dale had always been kind and loving and considerate, no matter what the doctors said. Now that Corrine had the opportunity to do the same for him, she devoted herself to his care. She resolved to stand by him no matter what, just the way he stood by her when she felt at her worst.

As the months passed, Dale slowly lost interest in almost everything that he enjoyed. His real estate business continued to falter until finally, in 1983, the family income dropped below $330 a month.

Two years later, Dale and Corrine filed for bankruptcy.

"Things will get better," Dale assured Corrine, although now he had to force himself to say the words. He was just so tired all the time.

Corrine was tired, too, and always wished she could do more. She remembered when they were young and robust. Who knew that thirty years later both of them would be in such poor health, that money would be so scarce?

She looked around at some of the couples they knew and saw marriages breaking up over much less than what she and Dale had been through. It made her so sad.

It wasn't that Corrine didn't understand how it felt to hit hard times. She did. She knew what it felt like to be frustrated and scared and confused and sometimes angry. But in spite of all that, she could never picture her life without her husband. Dale was the only man she'd ever loved.

Corrine could still see Dale the way he was when they met: seventeen years old, tall and skinny, with a rugged, outdoorsy look that appealed to her. The responsibility of all those years growing up on a farm gave him a maturity that she liked, too. He was the first guy she dated—and the last. Dale had been just as taken with her. He told his parents, his teachers, and anyone who would listen that he'd met the girl for him. She was sweet, soft-spoken, shy, and funny, and he didn't even care that she was two years older. She made his heart race.

Dale and Corrine had a strong foundation. Five children and more than thirty years later, they still loved each other very much. Corrine trusted her husband and had faith that they would make it. She found herself holding his hand more often.

Every night, they prayed.

The next few years were particularly trying. Dale struggled just to make it to work every day. His position at the company became tenuous and, eventually, began to slip through his fingers. One morning, in the spring of 1993, he finally hit bottom.

"Dale," his boss said, "could you come into my office please?"

"Sure."

Dale didn't know what he was about to hear, but as he stepped into the office and closed the door, he figured it wouldn't be good.

"Dale, we like you and you've been here for a long time," the boss began. "But your sales level isn't paying your desk cost for the office. It's to the point where our share of your commission isn't covering expenses, much less any profit."

"Are you firing me?"

"No, no," he said quickly, "not yet. But things have to change. If you don't start bringing in some money soon, we'll have to let you go."

So it had finally come to this.

Although the ultimatum hurt Dale deeply, it didn't surprise him. The worst part was that he had no idea what he'd tell his wife. Driving home, Dale thought of nothing but Corrine. What would she say? What would she think of him? Corrine had always been his rock, his greatest supporter. "But everyone has her limits," he worried. "She's been putting up with this for ten years."

Ten years. The realization that he'd been in the grip of a debilitating depression for a whole decade sent a jolt through his system. He'd lost so much time to a sickness that had slowly put a stranglehold on him and crippled almost every aspect of their lives.

When he walked in the front door, Corrine took one look at him and said, "What happened?"

"The boss gave me an ultimatum. He said I'd have to improve or they'll let me go. But Corrine, I can't do any better. I'm doing the best that I can."

Corrine took Dale's hand. "I know you are. And I know that you'll take care of this family the same way you always have. I trust you to make a living for us. We'll find a way and we'll be all right."

Dale could have cried with relief and gratitude. The fact that she was still willing to stand by him, in spite of everything that had happened, told him without a doubt that he was the luckiest man in the world.

Dale and Corrine made a decision. Dale left his job and started a new business from home fixing and selling Volvos.

"That way," he told his wife, "we'll still have some money

coming in and if I'm too sick to work only you and I will know about it."

For the next two years, Dale worked as hard as he could. But his hands and joints hurt all the time. He couldn't lift his right elbow above his shoulder. If he walked too much, his hips hurt. They got so inflamed that sometimes he couldn't get up or even sit down in a chair. Eventually he began hiring students whom he instructed to do the work that he could no longer manage.

Then one morning, while replacing a hose in a sedan, his left eye clouded over. Another fog had fallen and this one wasn't in his head. Everything began to blur.

"I'm going blind, Corrine!" he yelled, stumbling into the kitchen.

Corrine made an emergency appointment with an ophthalmologist, who told them that Dale was completely blind in his left eye and 50 percent blind in his right eye. The doctor referred them to a specialist who shed light on the mystery that had been plaguing them for so long.

"You have a tumor growing on your pituitary gland," the doctor told Dale. "It's thrown off your whole hormonal system, causing damage to your optic nerve, as well as the depression and physical ailments you've been experiencing. It's at least twelve years old. And it's big."

"Twelve years old!" thought Dale. "So that's what has been eating away at my life." He did a quick calculation and realized that twelve years ago was exactly when he'd first gone to the specialist who diagnosed him with low testosterone. If they had done a full battery of tests on him then, why, they probably could have caught this thing at the beginning! Suddenly, all his problems made sense.

"There's hope," he told Corrine. "They're gonna remove it and I'll be able to see again."

Right then, Corrine knew she had her husband back. After twelve long years.

They scheduled the surgery immediately to remove the tumor.

Before the operation, Dale and his wife prayed. Over the years, they had prayed for many things, including his and Corrine's health. Now he needed to talk to God more than ever.

"Thank you, God," Dale prayed. "Thank you for giving me a wife who has stood by me and supported me during times when many others would have walked away. She cared for me faithfully with kindness, understanding, and love. She never complained about money, though she could have in all those years that our income just kept dropping. She never complained about our lower standard of living or my ailing health. She never complained about my not working or called me lazy. She never accused me of losing ambition.

"And, Lord, the most important thing that she never did—she never doubted me.

"Thank you, God, for my wife Corrine. I am the luckiest man in the world."

Almost immediately after the surgery, Dale began to recover emotionally as well as physically. Miraculously, his eyesight also returned.

At his first checkup, his eye doctor told him that he had 20/20 vision in one eye and 20/50 vision in the other. "That's remarkable!" the doctor exclaimed.

"Why?" Dale asked.

"Didn't they tell you? When you've lost your eyesight to nerve damage, you don't get it back."

Dale's big, hearty laughter filled the doctor's office. "Nobody told me," he said. "I couldn't wait for the operation so I could see again!"

Corrine clasped his hand tightly and beamed.

"Now *that's* my husband," she said. "He's back."

Now, more than a decade after the surgery, Dale and Corrine sit next to each other in a back room of their small country church. "Never give up on your love," Dale says with a strong look in his eye. "Be steadfastly together. So much of our culture today is based on flash-in-the-pan, thrill-of-the-moment experiences. We need to understand that to commit to someone is to create a new life from which you never waver. When you are fully committed you'll find strength you didn't know you had."

"I always tell young women," Corrine says, "if you can live without him . . . don't marry him."

Stand By Me

Gerald and Opal Chavez
Married 44 years

"I have something to tell you," Francisco Chavez said to his new daughter-in-law. "Something important."

He motioned for Opal to move closer, then whispered two words in her ear, words in the strange guttural dialect that had been passed down through generation after generation by his Cochiti ancestors.

"I'm sorry," Opal said, trying not to let her frustration show. "But I don't understand."

Ever since Gerald had brought her home and introduced her to the other members of his tribe, she had been surrounded by this utterly foreign and, to her, incomprehensible language. She couldn't understand a thing anyone was saying, but the emotion behind the words came through crystal clear—they didn't like her and didn't approve of the marriage.

Except for Francisco. Gerald's father had been kind to Opal from the very beginning, and now he put his hand on her arm and gave her an encouraging smile.

"There are only two words you need to know," he said, then murmured the Cochiti phrase again. "That means 'wife of

Chavez.' Anytime you hear those two words it means they are talking about you."

Opal's eyes widened, and she repeated the phrase back to him, committing the two words to memory.

"Anytime you hear someone say them, I want you to stand up tall, and tell them, 'If you have anything to say about me, tell me so I can learn—because I can't learn if I can't understand what you are saying.' "

"I will," Opal promised, then gave her father-in-law an impulsive hug.

The words themselves may have been short, but the fact that Francisco taught them to her meant that Opal and Gerald had his support. And that was a very big thing indeed.

At the university in Chicago where Gerald and Opal went to school, all the Native American students were housed together in one building, all the various tribes sharing two floors of the YMCA, a short walk from campus. But that dormitory was the only place where tribal distinctions didn't matter.

Opal was a member of the Southern Cheyenne tribe of Oklahoma. Gerald was from the Cochiti Pueblo. As far as their families were concerned, they could have been from two different planets. It was practically unheard-of for members of different tribes to date, let alone marry. But Opal and Gerald didn't let that stop them.

They met in February of 1963 and fell in love at first sight.

"If there is such a term as 'soul mate,' that is what Gerald and I found in each other," Opal says. "Other people can feel and see the love between us. It is like we are two angels that were born with one wing apiece, and I can't fly by myself and he can't either. But if we hold onto each other, we can fly."

Opal knew that if her parents found out she was dating Gerald, they would ask her to come home and not see him anymore. So she told him that if he wanted to marry her, they had to do it then and there, and grow strong together, so their parents couldn't find any excuse for separating them.

On April 13, less than two months after they first met, Opal and Gerald both took the afternoon off from school, went down to the county courthouse, and got married.

But while getting married was easy, getting their tribes to accept their marriage wasn't. Although the young couple was fortunate to find an ally in Gerald's father, gaining the support of the rest of his tribe proved to be a lot harder.

"Excuse me," Opal said, then hesitated as the room grew quiet, a dozen hostile eyes turning to stare at her.

Opal had been minding her own business, helping wash dishes, while a group of women from Gerald's tribe laughed and gossiped behind her. But out of the flood of unfamiliar language swirling around her, her ears picked up two familiar words: the phrase her father-in-law had taught her, meaning "wife of Chavez." These women were gossiping about her!

Before she could stop herself, Opal turned and confronted the women. "Excuse me," she repeated, trying to keep her hands from shaking.

"I'm doing the best that I know how," she continued. "I don't know all the things that you do around here, but being here and washing dishes is my way to help. So if there is anything you need to teach me, say it so I can understand, because that is the only way I can learn."

Opal held her breath as everyone considered what she had said. Finally, the first person to speak was her father-in-law. "I'm so glad to have you married to my son!"

In time, Opal's warmth and intelligence won over the other members of Gerald's tribe. But then they still had to face the challenge of getting Opal's own tribe to accept Gerald.

They were so worried about her tribe's reaction, in fact, that they stayed in Chicago, putting off their visit until they felt that their marriage was strong enough to handle whatever her tribe threw at them.

Then one day, Opal received a letter from her aunt, inviting her and Gerald to come to Oklahoma for a ceremony for the Cheyenne Labor Day celebration.

When they arrived at the house, Opal's aunt led Gerald to a back bedroom. It was with trepidation that he followed her, but his worry disappeared when he saw the outfit that was laid across the bed. Opal's family had made a traditional tribal outfit for him.

"Today you are going to dance with us," they told him.

When they arrived at the ceremonial grounds, Opal's uncle led Gerald to the middle of the circle and addressed the tribe.

"This is our son-in-law. He is part of our family. So he is going to dance with us today."

Opal's tribe cheered, and Gerald and Opal beamed at each other.

"We want all the Cheyenne people to come and shake hands with him and welcome him not only into our family but into our tribe," her uncle continued. "This is the day we are introducing him into our circle."

All in all, it took eleven years for Opal and Gerald to build up the courage to go home. They had three children by then.

"In my area they prefer you marry the same tribe and the same with her. A Cheyenne marrying someone in the same tribe," Gerald explains.

"To keep continuity in the tribe," Opal adds, "and strength and stability in the tribe. There are a lot of traditions involved and they want us to pass down those traditions to our children, just as they were passed down to us."

"We had to make a decision early on," Gerald says, "what would come first: our commitment to tribal traditions or our commitment to our marriage?"

"Well, actually we always put God at the very top," Opal clarifies. "But then comes the commitment to our marriage. This doesn't mean you deny who you are or where you came from. You must treat the marriage like a newborn baby. Nurture it, give it a chance to grow, to become strong enough to withstand the pressures of the world."

"Protect your marriage," Gerald says. "Let nothing come between you and your spouse."

In their forty-three years of marriage, Opal and Gerald have passed a lot of traditions down to their children. Some come from the Cochiti tribe, others come from the Cheyenne. Some traditions are a blend of the two cultures.

Despite the difference in their backgrounds, Opal knew from the day she met him that Gerald would stand by her and

wouldn't compromise their relationship for anything. He knows she would do the same.

The most important tradition Gerald and Opal have passed down to their children?

Opal and Gerald look at each other and smile.

"Love."

Chapter 4

How Do You Keep the Romance Alive?

OLD FOGIES

—by Mat

If you ask me, a marriage without sex is the drive between St. Louis and Denver. Take a photo of a clod of dirt, tape it to the inside of your car window, then sit there and stare at it all day. The monotony is the same, minus the fuel bill. Fifteen hours of straight, flat roads through straight, flat fields surrounded by straight, flat horizons—the most boring trip known to mankind.

Research tells us that men have a sexual thought every five seconds, but I don't think that's necessarily true. Experience tells me it's actually more like every three seconds. Therefore, it's a little nerve-wracking to stand in line in the grocery store, bombarded by glossy magazine covers promising, "Re-ignite the Romance: 10 Tips Every Married Woman Needs to Know!" "What happened to the flame?" I've always wondered. "And what do you mean, *every* married woman?" When my friends complained about the arroyos of marital romance, I wanted to ask them: "How can that be? You've been married only two years!" It's like a sick joke, where someone says, "Hey, thirsty guy, go down this well and you'll have all the refreshing water you can drink for the rest of your life." So I finally commit to one well, drop in, and then discover all the water is dried up. (Hello . . . hello . . . hello. Can you hear me . . . me . . . me? Help . . . help . . . help.)

After all, if, as my married friends imply, physical intimacy decreases after just a few years, what would romance look like twenty, thirty, or even fifty years down the road? I had a sudden vision of Valentine's Day with my beloved, circa 2050: *She, in a dowdy housecoat and fuzzy slippers, watching game shows and downing the cheap chocolates she'd picked up for herself at the drugstore, knowing I'd forget, and me, head stuck in the fridge, rummaging around for another Natty Ice, belching loudly, patting my beer belly, and finally heading off to the den to catch some ESPN.* No! Stop! That could never happen to me, could it?

During our cross-country journey, we'd met a few couples who looked as if they'd rather link pinkies with Edward Scissorhands than with each other. And we'd also met couples bursting with affectionate vitality. Always a hand resting on the other's knee, a shared smile, and the unmistakable note of pride when they showed us their wedding pictures. "Most beautiful bride in the world," the husband would tell us, "and look at her. She still is." Yes, eighty-five-year-olds still blush.

A marriage with the flame burning five decades strong

sounded pretty wonderful to me. I longed to know the secret: What made one mature relationship sizzle while another went flat as a can of old beer? Jason and I had become pretty adept interviewers, but this question stumped us. We balked at asking our elders about physical intimacy. It felt rude, disrespectful, and really, really embarrassing. Think about it: Have you ever even *said* the word "sex" in front of your grandparents?

Thank goodness, the Marriage Masters, as if sensing our discomfort, began to set us straight. And what we learned surprised us: They told us that real intimacy stemmed from romantic friendship. Across the board, Marriages Masters said that sex, while an important part of marriage, is definitely not all-important. Physical intimacy waxed and waned. But in a great marriage, they said, romance never dies.

In other words, sex is the reward of building real romance, not the other way around. Real romance encompasses and transcends sex. They told us it's the intangible connection that draws them near and makes them yearn for closeness. One couple described romance as the spiritual unity they experience while watching the sun melt into the ocean; another, as the laughter that comes with a shared moment of joy. It's deeper and richer than simple sexual intimacy. It yields a greater connection and much more rewarding sex life. The path to this romance, the Marriage Masters told us, is not paved with hook-up sessions but with acts of friendship. Romance flourishes as a result of building friendship through fun times outside the bedroom. Fueling friendship ignites romance.

We met couples that found passion through dancing, skating, weekend getaways, and simply setting aside time each day just to be close to each other. Marriage Masters happily shared their fire-stoking secrets with us. We interviewed one husband and wife who both worked in the medical field and always struggled to find enough time together. But what they lacked in quantity, they made up for in quality. Every Tuesday, they would turn off their pagers, sneak next door to a symphony hall and share their love for classical music, listening to the orchestra practice for an hour. Another couple found true romance in their shared love for golf. For some reason sharing a physical activity together re-ignited their love life. (Hmm . . . anyone up for croquet?)

For sheer romantic energy, the prize goes to Carol and Mort Schomer of Florida, who'd been married fifty-six years. While we were in New York, Carol emailed us, hoping to rendezvous for a night on the town. "We are in Manhattan for one of our weeklong dancing trips," wrote Carol. "Mort and I want to show you young guys how seniors get down on the dance floor all night."

I was a bit skeptical, of course. All night? As in old fogey, lights out at ten o'clock all night? Regardless, Jason and I weren't about to pass up an opportunity to see a slice of the Big Apple's nightlife, while interviewing a couple. This was multitasking at its finest. We made a date with the Schomers: 9 P.M., Rainbow Room.

Atop the famed Rockefeller Plaza, sixty-five stories above Manhattan's sea of shining electricity, we stepped back in time. The Rainbow Room's live big-band orchestra set the mood with classic hits from yesteryear's greats like Glenn Miller, Eddy Duchin, Skinny Ennis, and Frank Sinatra. White-suited servers hustled between candlelit tables, which were arranged to take advantage of the panoramic views of New York's gloriously lit skyscrapers, including the Chrysler and Empire State buildings. In the center of it all, a slowly rotating dance floor beckoned. The place was majestic in its own right, but what really made it special that night were the two seventy-something lovers commanding the dance floor.

These two weren't doing the junior high sway—they were *dancing*.

With deft grace, Mort and Carol segued from the Lindy Hop to the Charleston, the jitterbug to the boogie-woogie, the tango to the LeRoc, then sneaked a *Saturday Night Fever* disco move in between. They had style to spare; no Gen Xers were as tuned in to each other as these two lovers. Mort, seventy-seven, was dressed in a dark and debonair pin-striped suit, handkerchief folded with a sharp peak, and splashy, two-toned spectator wing tips. At seventy-six, Carol was a glamour shot ready for the cover of *Fountain of Youth* magazine. Her sparkling earrings dangled from her curly red hair to her shoulders; her elegant black skirt was slit to the top of her thigh. They seemed to be extensions of each other: one leading, one following, both smiling—as they crossed the entire floor with Hucklebucks and other signature moves neither Jason nor I could imagine pulling off. They were fascinating to watch, partly because of their dazzling moves, partly because of their age, and mostly because of what they created with such fluidity on the dance floor: romance.

The band finished a set and we crossed the floor to shake hands and ask these vibrant Marriage Masters a few questions. For obvious reasons, our first was: "What's your secret to keeping your romance alive?"

"Common interests are so important to a happy marriage," Mort replied. "Dancing has been our thing since the day I pinned her in college. We go out six or seven nights a week and dance till closing time."

Carol gave us a sly smile. "That feeling goes home with us, too. We stay up till four or five in the morning, snuggled up watching old movies together in bed."

She patted Mort's thigh. "I don't know if other women my age feel as sensuous as I do. I can't get enough of this man."

"We like to take advantage of our times," Mort said. "Every minute. Tomorrow we'll cut a rug at the Tavern on the Green."

"Then we'll get a chance to show off our real dandies," Carol said, beckoning us over to their table. There, she showed us a photo album of them in the coolest outfits ever worn by man, senior or otherwise. Mort, for one, owned 150 pairs of shoes, 250 sport coats, 300 pairs of pants, and 100 belts, purchased mostly from thrift stores.

The band started a rendition of Sinatra's "New York, New York" and Mort gave Carol a look. She smiled. She knew. Just before they took the floor again, a thirty-something couple approached them and asked, "We just wanted to tell you that your dancing is phenomenal."

Mort gave them his winning grin.

"Is tonight your anniversary?"

"Nope," Carol replied.

The couple looked confused. "What are you celebrating then?"

The Schomers answered in unison: "The joy of life together."

Carol turned to us. "You've got to be best friends and lovers—that's the key."

With that, they linked arms tightly and returned to their own little rotating world.

By 1 A.M., Jason was resting his head on the photo album, and my head was pounding. "Music's kind of loud, don't you think?" I asked him.

Jason nodded. "I think I need some coffee," he said. "And I need to stretch."

"Or . . . it is pretty late. We could just, I don't know, call it a night?"

Mort and Carol slowed down long enough to say good-bye, then returned to the dance floor. They didn't want to miss the rest of the Swing.

While the couple later informed us they'd danced until 4 A.M., Jason and I got back to our hotel at 1:30 A.M. and collapsed into our beds. The old fogies that night turned out to be us.

How do you keep romance alive? The answer's not the least bit embarrassing. Just ask the Schomers. And the symphony goers . . . and the couples you are about to meet.

*Please Do Not Disturb:
Marriage in Progress*

Dorothy and Martin Meester
Married 47 years

She couldn't have imagined a more idyllic setting for the romantic getaway. The soft white sands felt like silk under her toes. A thin layer of clouds gathered harmlessly on the horizon, promising to take part in a stellar sunset soon to come. Emerald green

waves rolled in, breaking rhythmically and peacefully on the pristine shores. There wasn't another soul in sight and, best of all, she was in the strong arms of her man—the picture-perfect beach would be all theirs to explore.

She noticed a large conch shell, something she'd never seen outside tourist shops, and her man picked it up and raised it to her ear, whispering, "Listen to this, baby . . ."

Beep! Beep! Beep!

5:30 A.M.! The alarm clock ripped Dorothy back to reality. "Oh please, God, that was so good," she moaned, throwing back the covers, pushing her feet to the cold floor. "I liked the sand better."

Martin, her husband, hummed The Who's "See Me, Feel Me" in the shower. As she brushed her teeth, she looked upon his five-foot-nine soapy silhouette through the opaque glass. "It'd be nice . . ." Her thought trailed off into a sigh. She looked back at herself in the mirror. "Oh, how the years go by," she mused. Spit. Rinse. Flush.

"Morning, baby," Martin sang.

"Morning, honey," she sang back. "Breakfast is on the way."

Fifteen minutes later, Martin arrived in the kitchen and sat down for a freshly brewed cup of coffee and a plate of bacon and eggs over easy—his favorite. He was wearing his brown business suit, complete with the ugly bright green fish tie his oldest daughter had given him for Father's Day—a sentimental favorite. Dorothy started to tell him about her dream: "I had a perfect dream last night—"

"Oops, six-thirty!" Martin said, grabbing his jacket off the back of the chair. "Gotta go."

Dorothy picked up a brown paper bag. "Don't forget your"— he snagged it before she finished— "lunch."

Standing in the doorway, the carpool gang honking every twenty seconds, Martin gave Dorothy a quick kiss and patted her fanny. "Have a great day, baby."

"Hey!" she exclaimed.

"What?"

"Well . . . don't stop," she said, moving into him, close enough to smell his Old Spice and—

Honk!

"Okay, I really gotta go," he said, "but save that perfect dream for our fifteen, okay? I want to hear about this." He dashed out the door and down the sidewalk to the waiting car.

Dorothy stood in the doorway, empty-handed. "Bye."

She closed the door and snapped instantly into Mom mode. "Okay, kids!" she announced, hustling up the stairs. "Rise and shine and give God the glory, glory!"

From bedroom to bedroom, she made the rounds, clicking on lights and singing her standard wake-up greetings.

"Up and at 'em, boys!"

Surrounded by posters of Elvis Presley and the Beach Boys and Joe Montana, Stephen, fifteen, and Rick, thirteen, rolled over in their beds, groaning, "Do we have to go to school today?"

"Good morning, girls!"

Yolanda, eight, and Rachel, nine, flumped out of their princess-themed bunk beds and stumbled into the bathroom.

Down the hall, Dorothy flicked on the light in the last bedroom. Romana, ten, the sleepyhead of the crew, never wanted to wake up. After gently tickling the fleshy pads on her feet, Dorothy pulled Romana out of bed by the ankles until she stood, half asleep, swaying in the middle of her room. "Get some clothes on and come down for breakfast," Dorothy said.

A train of children, sluggish Romana manning the caboose, thundered down the stairs in their clean school clothes and filled the five empty chairs at the large oblong kitchen table. Arms crisscrossed over the table to reach for milk. Eggs. Toast. Butter.

An extra napkin to soak up the spilt orange juice. Silverware and plates clanked. Half-full talking mouths interrupted one another. Within fifteen minutes, five kids were fed and five brown bag lunches were filled, tailored to each child's preferences: white bread, wheat bread, ham, tuna, turkey, peanut butter and jam, apples, bananas, oranges, 10 cents for milk, and, of course, a little "I love you" note at the bottom that they will discover while among their classmates. Dorothy chuckled at the thought of their mortification.

By half past seven, Dorothy had all five kids piled in the van, fighting the morning school traffic packed with minivans and moms as she dropped Stephen off at the high school, then Rick and Romana at the middle school, and finally Rachel and Yolanda at the grade school.

Back home, Dorothy gazed at the disaster zone in front of her. Pens, colored pencils, watercolors, toy cars and trucks, paper dolls, puzzles, board games, and random shoes lay scattered across the family room. Half-filled glasses of milk and plates with dried egg yolk cluttered the countertops, pots and pans soaked in soapy water and puddles of orange juice hid under the kitchen table. Dirty towels and stinky clothes spilled out of the laundry bin.

After the kitchen, Dorothy started in on the mountain of laundry. With a pile of folded towels on the bed, a load in the washer, and a load drying, Dorothy jumped in the shower. Under the steaming water she revisited her romantic getaway: the silky sand, the gentle waves, Martin's strong arms, the smile and kiss. She reveled in the idea of no responsibilities, no distractions, no appointments, no errands to run, no kids pulling at her clothes or asking her what time dinner will be—just uninterrupted time alone with her Martin.

With a towel wrapped tightly around her head, she looked at the clock. "Shoot . . . I'm late," she thought.

Dorothy barely had enough time to hit the grocery store before picking up the kids from school and shuttling them to their respective sporting activities, each on a different field on an opposite side of town. After racing all over the burbs and back home again, Dorothy pulled out a freshly washed pan from the cabinet and filled it with her special meat loaf. She popped it in the oven and hopped back in the car to pick up her five sweaty, dirt-caked kids from their sports. Once home, the kids kicked off their muddy cleats by the garage door, ran upstairs, and threw their stinky clothes in the hamper, refilling it to the brim.

At 6:30, Martin came through the door, sentimental fish tie loose around his neck. "I'm home!" he called out.

Dorothy met him halfway in the family room with a scotch and water in one hand, a glass of white wine in the other. She leaned in and gave him a soft kiss.

"Groooss!" Romana said, standing at the top of the stairs.

The three girls scampered down the stairs, talking at the same time about their day.

"Dad, I want to show you what I made at school today!" Romana exclaimed.

"No, Dad, listen to what happened to me," countered Rachel.

Not one to be left out, Yolanda pleaded, "Daaad, I need to tell you something. . . ."

"Girls, you know the rule," Dorothy said.

"I wanna hear all about my princesses' day in just a little bit," Martin said, "but my fifteen minutes with the queen comes first."

Martin and Dorothy, hand in hand, headed upstairs.

Stephen, sitting at the kitchen table, whispered to Rick, "There they go again for a little Mom and Dad sex time."

Rick grimaced. "Disgusting."

Locking the bedroom door behind her, Dorothy lit a candle and turned on the radio. Martin shed his suit and put on some comfortable khakis and a T-shirt. He flopped onto the bed and patted the empty space next to him. Dorothy snuggled up to his side, laying her head on his shoulder, her hand caressing his chest. They both took a deep breath and exhaled together, the first satisfied sigh of the day.

"How are you, honey?" he asked.

"Lovely now." She smiled.

"So tell me about this dream."

"Oh my, it was beautiful, so perfect. We were all alone on this tropical beach. . . ."

Martin laughed as she described the seashell-turned-alarm-clock. "You poor thing," he said. Then he put his hand up to Dorothy's ear and whispered, "Listen to this, baby: *Wissshheer-rewiisshh.*"

Dorothy giggled, pulling her ear away from his tickling lips. "What the heck is that?"

"It's the ocean surf inside the shell." He laughed, then tried again: *"Wiierrewwwiisshh."*

Dorothy tried her best seashell sound—*"sssshhhhheeeehhhhe-heh"*—but couldn't stop giggling. Martin was howling, almost falling off the bed.

Their laughter drifted upstairs to the kids' rooms, where Stephen was jabbering to Rick and Rick was covering his ears, and where the girls were spilling paints and drawing unicorns and otherwise making new messes for their mother to eventually clean. For the remaining twelve minutes of their daily ritual, contrary to Stephen's forensic assessment, Dorothy and Martin kept their clothes on and simply enjoyed their time alone. They shared details about their day: the stress, the errands, the funny moments. They sipped their drinks and relished their uninterrupted connection. As the alone time expired, they embraced tightly and said "I love you," looking into each other's eyes like young lovers.

On their way back into the front lines of parenthood and a dinner table full of reaching arms and funny stories of the day, Dorothy opened up the bedroom door just as Martin gave her one last kiss, an extra-warm one this time.

"Grooosss!" yelled Romana.

Now a widow of eight years, Dorothy's memories of those daily one-on-ones with Martin are especially bittersweet.

She sits at the same large table that had once held so many family meals, talking about a recent discussion with her daughter Romana. "She told me what they'd all thought Martin and I were doing with our fifteen minutes." She laughs whimsically. "I guess I can't fully deny it, but the most important part of those little slices of daily time together was the connection we created, all the little things like holding each other, laughing and being silly together.

"In the end, it's the little things, when done often, that will make the biggest difference in a marriage's romantic life. . . ." She pauses, smiling coyly. "Now that he's gone, I just wish I hadn't had so many 'headaches.' "

"Stardust"

Pearl and Al Stone
Married 50 years

"Can you believe it's been forty years?" Al asked, clinking his cocktail glass against Pearl's. "Just saying that makes me feel old."

"You can get old by yourself, Grandpa, but not me," she teased, smiling.

"Whatever." Al took a sip of his screwdriver and winked at his wife. "You'll always be a year older than me, sweetie."

Pearl playfully slapped at his arm, sputtering with mock outrage. Al had been teasing her for the past forty years about the difference in their ages; it was hopeless to think he'd stop now, even if it was their anniversary.

As Al signaled to a passing waiter for another round, Pearl got up from her chair. "Be right back," she said.

She wended her way through the crowded bar, skirting the edge of the dance floor as she headed toward the ladies' room. The place was packed, and deservedly so. A seven-piece band had the guests of the Poconos Summit Resort jumping as it played a set list of hits from the '40s and '50s.

Al's foot tapped with the beat as he watched his wife cross the room. But the instant she disappeared into the ladies' room and the door shut behind her, he jumped up.

He walked up to the edge of the stage and motioned to the bandleader, who leaned down to talk to him.

Al gave the man his most charming grin. "I was wondering if you could do something for me. . . ."

In the ladies' room, Pearl finished touching up her lipstick, then gave herself one last appraising glance in the mirror.

"Not bad," she thought, "all things considered . . ."

Pearl was always a little surprised whenever she caught sight of herself—in her mind, she was still the same nineteen-year-old girl who had first met Al forty years earlier at the Plainfield roller rink in New Jersey. She felt so young inside that whenever she glanced in a mirror, she ended up being startled by the sixty-year-old face looking back at her.

She gave her hair one final pat, then turned and headed back out to the bar where Al was waiting for her.

But the instant she set foot out of the ladies' room, the spotlight from the stage hit her.

She froze, confused, and her bewilderment grew when the bandleader leaned into his microphone and asked, "Are you Pearl Stone?"

"Yes . . . ?"

Pearl could see Al standing alone in the center of the now-empty dance floor, beaming as the bandleader picked up his baton and motioned to the band.

"Then in honor of your fortieth anniversary, this song's dedicated to you," he said.

The band started to play, and chills ran up and down Pearl's spine.

And now the purple dusk of twilight time . . .

Pearl's smile stretched from ear to ear as she moved to the dance floor, where her husband was waiting for her. Al held out his hand and she took it.

Dozens of eyes fixed on Al and Pearl as they danced, cheek to cheek, to "their song."

But Pearl saw only Al.

She tightened her arms around him as they swirled across the dance floor, utterly content to share this moment with the only other person in the world who fully understood what it meant.

Candles illuminated the corners of the small attic apartment where Pearl and Al lived, bathing the room in a golden glow. An empty bottle of wine sat next to plates of abandoned hors d'oeuvres on the coffee table.

Al leaned back on one of the large, fluffy cushions on the floor, his arm draped across his bride's shoulders.

Pearl rested her head on Al's shoulder and held her wineglass in the air, admiring the gold wedding band on her newly adorned finger.

The attic windows muffled the bustling city sounds. The noise of honking cars, pedestrians whistling for taxis, and sweeping store owners was faintly audible in the background as Al and Pearl enjoyed a thousand conversations about nothing.

Their words, strung together like links in a chain, meandered through hours of time.

The automatic arm on the record player lifted the needle for the tenth time that evening and set it back down at the beginning of the record. Pearl and Al fell silent, their conversation pausing once again as the sounds of cinematic strings and Nat King Cole's honeyed voice serenaded the two lovers on the floor. That night was the first time in their lives they had ever heard "Stardust," and they felt like they could listen to the song forever.

And now the purple dusk of twilight time . . .

The candles burned down to nothing as Pearl and Al listened to "Stardust" over and over and over again.

"Honey," Pearl said suddenly, sitting up, "this is *our* song."

Al closed his eyes, absorbing the music. "All right. This is our song."

He stood up and held out his hand.

"What are you doing?" asked Pearl.

"C'mon."

Pearl took his hand. Al helped her up, pulling her close. Eyes closed, cheek to cheek, Pearl and Al slowly danced to the music. The entire city dissolved away—the cars driving by, the people walking on the sidewalk, the clerk sweeping in front of his convenience store all faded into the background as they danced, lost in their own private world.

Over the next few years, Pearl and Al played "Stardust" so many times the grooves on the record wore thin. The song really, truly was *theirs*; at the sound of the opening notes, they sought out each other's arms.

Pearl and Al liked to go roller skating on Monday nights at the rink where they had first met. And whenever "Stardust" played over the ancient, crackly PA system, they dropped whatever they were doing and skated together.

Many days, Al was at the counter of the snack bar, in the middle of ordering two sodas and two vanilla ice creams, when he'd hear "Stardust" come through the speakers. He'd leave in the middle of his order and look for Pearl on the rink.

Al's right hand would gently wrap around Pearl's petite waist, his left hand warmly embracing hers. They'd glide into their own private world, a world no one knew but them. In a room with hundreds of people, Pearl and Al became the only two in the universe as they skated to their song.

"Stardust" was playing when Al kissed Pearl good-bye before heading to Fort Bragg to serve his country, and it was playing when he finished his service and returned home. In between, Pearl played the record constantly; it was the only way she knew to make the pain of missing him subside for a bit. When "Stardust" was playing, she could shut her eyes and imagine that Al was hearing it too, and wherever he was and whatever he was doing, he'd set down his gun or abandon his tank in the middle of the training field and take her in his arms.

"Stardust" played when they signed the papers to buy their first real house together, and it played while they packed up the tiny attic apartment where they had started their marriage. It played when Pearl and Al heard the news that they were about to become parents, and it played when they became grandparents, and then great-grandparents.

On holidays, the entire family would gather around the organ in the family room of the house and sing along as Pearl played Christmas carols.

But somewhere between "Joy to the World" and "Silent Night," Pearl would pull out the sheet music to "Stardust." Al would sit down on the piano bench next to her, and he'd sing while she played.

The rest of the family would fall silent as Pearl and Al played their song. And no matter how many family members were gathered around them, they always felt the same way they did the first time they heard it. The kids would fade into the background, the presents and gaily colored wrapping paper and delicious scents of pine and cinnamon and the turkey roasting in the oven for Christmas dinner would disappear, and Pearl and Al would be aware of nothing in the world except each other.

At the Poconos Summit Resort, the bandleader finished crooning the last few lines of "Stardust," and the audience burst into applause. But even though the dance was over, Pearl and Al kept their eyes shut and their arms around each other, savoring the last few moments of their song.

None of the other people in the crowded bar knew what the song signified, no one else could begin to understand what it meant to them.

They had listened to their record until they wore it out. Pearl had played the song on the organ so often that the sheet music was yellow and tattered, transparent in spots from being pulled out so much. But despite this, the song had endured, the way their love had endured.

Whenever they heard it, no matter where they were or who was playing it, whether they were apart or together, alone or surrounded by loved ones or strangers, Pearl and Al were instantly transported back to the tiny attic room where they heard it the first time. The opening notes would play, and they would find each other and move into each other's arms, with eyes for no one but each other.

"It's like 'Stardust' is the soundtrack to our marriage," Al says, sitting next to Pearl on the front steps of their large home in rural New Jersey.

Pearl leans playfully into her man. "Romance is making memories—the kind of memories that only the two of you understand. What I love about marriage is the private world that Al and I get to share. Find something that is just yours and never let it go, that's how you keep the romance alive."

Mission: Impossible

Jerry and Dena Robbins
Married 49 years

Countdown to B-day. Jerry reviewed his itinerary and thought, "This is going to be the best one yet!" Dena, his wife of forty-two years, was turning sixty, and Jerry had pulled out all the stops. He wanted to show Dena how much he loved her, and a blender or even a bottle of perfume just wouldn't do. Jerry had seen Dena look at herself in the mirror lately and frown. Yes, they were both getting older, but didn't the woman realize she looked even lovelier now than when they'd met as teenagers? Back then, of course, Jerry hadn't thought about keeping the romance alive.

Young love, inherently ardent and heady, had a momentum all its own. Over the decades, however, keeping marriage romantic required nurturing, finesse and, to Jerry's way of thinking, a keen imagination. His plan for Dena's sixtieth, months in the making, featured a myriad of players and spanned three states. Under his direction, the birthday extravaganza would unfold flawlessly over the next two days.

But the next morning, when a well-dressed stranger showed up at Dena's office, announcing, "I've been instructed to ask you to accompany me," Dena refused to go.

"Surely you jest," she snapped.

Her visitor smiled inscrutably. "I have a letter that I was instructed to give you, in case you had any questions." He pulled out an envelope. It read, "Mission: Impossible."

By this time, Dena's coworkers had gathered at her door, listening attentively. Dena read aloud from the typed page: " 'Mrs. Robbins: Tomorrow is a very important day. . . . You have been assigned a very difficult and dangerous mission! The man who delivered this note will drive you to a meeting with a person who, with a specially trained "team" of experts, will assist you. Should you choose not to accept . . . this note will self-destruct in five seconds, and a man very well-known to you will be in deep caca.' "

Aha! That husband of hers! At least Dena assumed this was her husband's handiwork. The note was unsigned.

Dena looked at her employer, Sharon, who had promised her a pre-birthday lunch at Philadelphia's finest restaurant. They had 11:30 A.M. reservations. "Go with him," Sharon urged, trying to hide a smile. The luncheon had been a ruse. Jerry had enlisted

Sharon's help to ensure, one, that his wife would make no other plans that would interfere with his own, and two, that Dena would dress up for work that day. Sharon had even gone so far as to advise the birthday girl to save room for a selection from the restaurant's famed dessert tray. Dena had skipped breakfast in anticipation.

So off she went, reminding her still-nameless escort to return her in time for her luncheon date. The taciturn fellow nodded and led her outside to a black limousine, one of those stretch models that reminded Dena of a senior class on prom night.

"Oh, Jerry," she thought, ready to . . . but wait! Stepping inside the luxury transport, Dena found herself alone. Where was Jerry? And where were they going? The route made no sense to Dena. Ten minutes later, the limo doubled back, pulling up to a hotel about a block and a half from Dena's office. Smiling and waving, her husband emerged from the lobby, bounded down the steps, and hopped inside the limo beside his startled wife.

"Where are we going? When will we be back?" the barrage began. Then the reminder: "I have a lunch date." And finally: "Where *are* we going?"

Jerry smiled. "Dear, you remember our first vacation?"

Dena gulped. They had rented a cabin at Lake Wallenpaupack in the Poconos. How could she forget those cabins with holes for windows? And the entertainment! Polka dancing to accordion music. "That place was horrible!" she thought. Jerry must be teasing, right?

Then the limo swung onto the New Jersey Turnpike, better known to Dena as the road to Manhattan, and she settled down, but only momentarily. "I didn't pack!" she said. "What about . . ."

Jerry revealed that the trunk of the limo contained almost the entire contents of their bathroom and a selection of Dena's best clothes. She should have known. Jerry did everything with a flourish but never overlooked the details. Take their twenty-fifth wedding anniversary, which featured a renewing of vows designed to compensate for the ceremony they missed when they were young and broke. To commemorate two and a half decades of marriage, Dena wore an antique white dress, Jerry, a white tux and tails. Their three sons, similarly attired, also wore top hats. During the recessional, the wedding party marched and high-stepped to the song "One" from *A Chorus Line.*

What did Jerry have in store for her now? Finally, the limo pulled up to the white and gold canopy outside the spectacular Pierre Hotel on New York's Fifth Avenue.

Dena and Jerry had barely settled into their suite overlooking Central Park when one bellman arrived with flowers, then another, bearing fruit. Jerry's packing job was near perfect, she noticed, save for the absence of her foundation and his idea of suitable footwear.

"You expect me to walk in New York in these?" she asked, holding up a pair of four-inch heels.

"I think they're sexy." He shrugged.

That night, the couple dined at the Four Seasons and listened to a favorite singer at Café Carlyle.

The next morning, Dena awakened early and slipped out of bed to watch the sunrise over Central Park. Sensing her absence, Jerry woke up and joined her. As the city emerged from the darkness, he sang one of their favorite songs, "When You Were

Sixteen," and read a poem he had written for her. His eyes filling
with tears, he read:

> *You can pretend that you're twenty-nine—*
> *What's the difference?*
> *When I look at you,*
> *I see a beautiful young girl of seventeen*
> *That I met on the beach in Atlantic City . . .*

> *You're cute*
> *You're sassy*
> *You're bold*
> *You're classy . . .*

> *You're a good mother*
> *You're a good cooker*
> *You're a great lover*
> *You're a fabulous looker . . .*

> *You're loving*
> *You're divine*
> *And today*
> *You're (let's pretend) twenty-nine*

Then Jerry told Dena she had another mission to fulfill: shopping. This delicate assignment would require cunning and patience on his part, for Jerry hated shopping. Dena's sartorial
indecisiveness drove him crazy. So spending a day deep in the

belly of Manhattan boutiques with his sweetheart was a precious gift indeed.

And yet, Jerry had a wonderful time. He was so pleased to have arranged something Dena would enjoy. Customarily, his wife hunted for bargains, but this time, Jerry insisted she simply buy what she wanted. He thrilled to her happiness. Dena felt so cherished. It was like the time he had accompanied her to her weekend-long class reunion, where Jerry didn't know anyone. "Weren't you bored?" Dena had asked him afterward. No, Jerry told her. He said he'd had a wonderful time just observing her happiness. Today, Dena realized the biggest gift was not the new outfits, but her husband. "Everyone likes to hear, 'I love you,'" Dena thought. "But showing your love means more."

At the end of the second day, Dena received a final note: "You and your 'team' have successfully completed your 'mission.' The 'goods' will arrive in Philadelphia. After all, WHY SHOULD YOU SCHLEP???" The evening ended with dinner and a show.

Once home, Dena told all her friends about the incredible trip and her wonderful husband, although her friends' husbands were less than thrilled. "How come you don't . . . ?" "Why can't you ever . . . ?" Their wives gave them an earful. Jerry had little sympathy for the beleaguered spouses. After all, he knew that keeping romance alive is not an impossible mission, even after decades of marriage. Imagination, humor, and avoidance of all things humdrum matter far more than money.

"Romance is about doing the unexpected," Dena says. "Make sure you keep a little mystery in your marriage."

"We'll be walking down the street in public," adds Jerry, "and all of a sudden I'll give her a real big kiss—a real smacker—a movie-star kind of kiss. She never knows when it's going to happen. Now that's romantic!"

Mission: Accomplished.

Chapter 5

How Do You Bring an "It'll Do" Marriage Back to "I Do!"?

IT'LL NOT DO

— by Jason

Success is always in the eye of the beholder, but I found a true reference point for "average" during our nationwide interview tour's fourteen-hour overnight haul to Dallas. We were exhausted and considering a stop . . . cautiously. I know the songs say good things about the heart of Texas, but it seemed to me that the ominous prairie expanses out there harbored only three things in depth: rabid prairie dogs, ghost towns, and haunted roadside motels. Maybe I just needed some sleep, but stars big and bright be damned, things out there looked downright shady.

One motel in particular begged for a wrecking ball. The building's paint had stripped more than a Vegas dancer. The "view rooms" would have been pleasant, I'm sure, with the amazing things they'd done with the weed garden outside. Of course, views of anything would've proven difficult, since most of the windows were either boarded up or dressed with curtains resembling thick cheesecloth. My favorite part was the motel's sign, hand-painted on the exterior of the building in huge, yellow block letters: The It'll Do Motel.

That, to me, said a lot about our cross-country trip. Don't get me wrong; the meetings with the Marriage Masters were getting better and better. We were meeting couples from all walks of life, comparing West Coast marriages to East Coast and everything in between, and generally getting an excellent snapshot of the diversity in American marriages.

But in the areas of road tripping itself, of living a free-spirited, vagabond lifestyle, the trip wasn't going quite as I'd planned. Maybe my expectations were a little lofty. I got on the road thinking we'd be a daring, rough-around-the-edges pair of treasure-hungry sailors, scurrying around the nation's backwaters in a boat on wheels that begged to be swerved astray. Wherever memorable, mischievous adventures were to be found, we'd be found there, too. My heart was prepped for that moment I'd cross paths with a beautiful wild woman in torn Levi's and a Stetson hat, a fine spelling bee champion in her own right, hitchhiking on a desolate stretch of old Route 66. I'd slow the RV down next to her, Tchaikovsky's *1812 Overture* playing on the tape deck, and tell her that we were on our way to meet a legendary gun-toting, four-letter-word-slinging Marriage Master couple who'd started their own high-powered cognac operation up in the Oklahoma mountains. Without a second thought, she'd respond, "I couldn't think of one thing better to do with my life than take that journey with you, Jason." Then we'd drift off to wherever the wind wanted to take us.

But none of that happened. Meeting with Marriage Masters was a tiring business, and the sights we'd been so determined to see while planning the tour—Mat's "Touchdown Jesus" in South Bend, Grandma Dorothy's Virginia plantation home, and my Niagara Falls—were all ditched for an hour or two of extra sleep.

So while the road trip part was good, it wasn't as great as it could've been. I'd resigned myself to the fact that the road trip part of it wasn't going to be much fun, and that was that.

A month or two of crummy road life I can handle. Though I might wake up covered in bedbugs, I'd probably survive a night in a Texas roadside motel. But a lifetime in a mildly acceptable, average marriage would be a slow, torturous death for me. I shuddered at the thought of waking up next to my wife after fifteen years with the sudden realization that our marriage was deep asleep. That the connection and the zest we'd shared for each other when saying "I do" were stuck in a hibernation from which neither of us knew how to wake. Or worse, that neither of us felt capable of restoring the passion! An *It'll do* marriage just won't do for me. I want my wife and me to thrive on the highest levels of connection. I want us to be one.

Here's what bothered me, though: That's what everyone wants, isn't it?

Nobody honeymoons at the It'll Do Motel. But the occupancy rate is pretty dang high. It seems to me that most people enter marriage with high hopes. After all, an entire industry has been built around the anticipation of that momentous occa-

sion. With all that wedding hoopla—the bridal shows, bridal magazines, theme showers, china patterns, toaster ovens, place settings, his and hers monogrammed towels, for heaven's sake— marriage ought to live up to its advance billing, right? It should not be a fancy wrapped package with ribbons and bows and no gift inside.

Yet every year, misty-eyed couples take the aisle walk only to be sorely disappointed down the road. I'm not even talking about the one in two marriages that ends in the divorce. What scares me are the marriages that started out with such high hopes only later to find themselves with sagging walls and a caved-in roof.

For example, one of my friends begged us to meet her aunt and uncle, a couple she described as having "*the* perfect marriage."

"Forty-nine years together and I've never once heard them exchange a harsh word," she said.

An hour with the couple revealed the secret to their absence of acrimony: They exchanged very few words whatsoever. When the aunt spoke, her husband fiddled with his watch or gazed out the window. When he talked, she cut him off. He didn't object; she was speaking again, so it was his cue to look out the window again.

Yet to my friend, this couple epitomized bliss. Maybe they were just having an off day. Or, maybe, a marriage without blowups constituted a match made in heaven.

Mat sat through one meeting so awkward and disturbing he finally asked the couple why they had stayed together. For an entire hour, they had berated one another, as if Mat were a divorce court judge divvying up the assets. Still, they found his question puzzling. "Because we're married, of course," they answered.

Their answer made me think back to all the times I'd eaten dinner at my friends' homes, and the parents would ask us about school but barely glance at each other. I thought about a beach trip with a friend's family one spring vacation during college. The parents didn't argue or interrupt each other. The husband automatically handed his wife the business section of the paper over breakfast each morning. They consulted each other about the weather forecast. But in that whole week, I never saw them touch—not even a hand brushing a shoulder or forearm, nothing. He was a jogger; she favored walking. The Pacific Ocean in all its glory lay just a few hundred yards from their doorstep, but never once did the two of them venture down to the beach together. My buddy never complained about his parents. He was the product of a "happy" family. The message I was starting to get was: Marriage isn't exciting. Marriage isn't bliss. Marriage is getting by.

But through Project Everlasting, I was getting a different message. I was meeting couples who were so emotionally intimate, so mutually inclusive, and so exemplary that a very single twenty-eight-year-old guy like me with a lock on his heart closed his eyes midinterview, thinking, "My Lord, I've been missing out on something. There is excitement. There is bliss."

The Marriage Masters laid it all out for me. Doesn't matter what generation you're talking about, they said, couples go into marriage with high expectations. They envision matrimony as a continuation of the romantic adventure that began with their wedding. Then reality sets in: bills to pay, diapers to change, dinner to put on the table, a house to clean, a job that sends you home stressed and tired. The burdens of everyday life put wear and tear on a marriage and kind of take over.

I was surprised to learn that many of the inspiring Marriage Masters had "It'll do" periods in their relationships, too. There were times when the marriage stagnated or drifted, when the couple became so caught up in tending to career, kids, or crisis they forgot to tend to their marriage. They communicated the business of the day, they scheduled dinner and the kids' dentist's appointments, and figured out who would pick up the dry cleaning, but they didn't connect. The relationship became less nuanced, more routine. Come-hither glances wilted. They stopped touching. Seeing the disappointment in my face, one older gentleman we were interviewing commented, "What? You think fifty years together and we never hit a lull? Never got into a rut? Son, you've got a lot to learn about marriage."

In a nutshell, what they taught me is this: Each "It'll do" phase in the relationship was preceded by decreased communication, especially the heartfelt, meaningful kind. And each time that happened, either husband or wife or both eventually recognized the lapse and found a way to revitalize the communication. They shared more, opened up, and grew closer as a result. And that's the difference between an "It'll do" marriage and an "I do!" one.

And while our Marriage Masters may drop in at the It'll Do Motel every now and then, you can be sure they won't be staying long. That's what makes them Marriage Masters.

Rock the Boat
David and Marylin Geiger
Married 49 years

"We were married singles," David says. "Two people living in the same house, but with two independent lives."

"There wasn't anything to talk about at the end of the day," admits his wife, Marylin. "It's not that we were running around on each other. We just weren't together."

"I barely knew who she was anymore."

"And vice versa. We were heading in very separate directions."

The way the Geigers describe their early days of marriage, one can't help but suspect a slight exaggeration, perhaps a storyteller's flourish. Now married forty-nine years, their connection is electric, nothing like the flickering bulb it seems to have been at year fifteen. Today they communicate like pros. David gives Marylin his full attention while she explains her perspective. Whenever he has something to add or argue (not a rare event), he asks for permission to interject. Marylin, too, is in tune to David's storytelling. She knows just when to take the baton, to add a detail without disrupting his flow. They are vocal and opinionated, yet respectful at the same time. They seem to know each other throughout. They have a rhythm. It's a rhythm that's taken them decades of practice to achieve—practice that was rarely perfect in the beginning.

What began as a charming story between two next-door neighbor kids who fell in love talking over a fence had become a story about a husband and wife whose marriage had succumbed to . . . well, life.

Day in and day out, Marylin fought Long Island traffic for an hour to her shift at an art gallery. On the way home, she'd sit through another hour of traffic, stop at the market to pick up groceries, and dash from the car to the kitchen to whip up dinner for her family. David would work sixteen hours at his start-up business, eat a quick evening meal with his family, then squeeze ten minutes of homework time in with his kids before collapsing into bed. It was a harried, all-consuming routine for both. Memories of cruising in David's hot rod '49 Chevy convertible and listening to Ravel's *Boléro* under the stars, or sitting on the couch watching Fernandel and Jaques Tati films till the wee hours of the night were just that: memories, bits of nostalgia left over from the brighter days of marriage.

But the daily grind was only half the problem. David also developed a love affair down by the docks with a gorgeous dame named the *Sea Hunter.* Normally, David finished work at ten o'clock at night, but on the special occasion when he did finish early, the first thing he'd think to do was to take the twenty-three-foot fishing boat out to sea for a couple of hours of peace. He'd drop by the house to give Marylin a quick kiss, grab some fishing gear and garb, then head out to the Atlantic. Out there, no customers complained about his products, no employees argued pensions and vacation time and company cars, no wife interrupted his already stressful workday with irritating questions: "How do I get the dishwasher repaired?" "I'm across town—can you come fix my flat tire?" "What should I do about Adam? He just told me a lie and I told him he'd need a time-out and now he's throwing a temper tantrum." Out there, he found a way to remain sane.

His lonely counterpart at home, however, was having a hard time maintaining her sanity. Consistently being blown off for a hunk of floating fiberglass was not Marylin's idea of a solid marriage. She was frustrated that the few opportunities they did have to connect were squandered. If it wasn't the fishing boat, then it was a party with friends or a weekend flick at the theater—not exactly fountainheads for intimate "How do you feel about us lately?" moments. She had known from day one that David would be no Casanova husband. After all, he'd proposed to her at one o'clock in the morning—over the phone—from a ski cabin three hours away, then gone on to present her an engagement ring—wrapped in a crumpled brown paper bag—with the less than romantic acknowledgment: "Here's something you might like." He'd never been the emotional type, no reciting love haikus while a long-stemmed rose dangled from his lips. Not that Marylin had delusions about it; rather, his fortitude was a major reason she'd fallen in love with him.

Still, a heartfelt conversation here and there might have been nice.

On the heels of the '50s and '60s "doting, darling wife" and "silent, sturdy husband" marriage model, Marylin heard many of her female friends struggling in the same "stuck" relationship. Men were tough. Men provided. Men didn't have the time, energy, inclination, or role models to know how to open up and emotionally connect to their wives. Her friends were putting up with it. Marylin couldn't. She needed David to talk to her. She wanted to know him on the deepest levels. She wanted more out of the man with whom she'd chosen to share a bed, a family, a lifetime.

David's response? "I don't know what you're talking about. We don't fight, there's food on the table, and we love each other. Our marriage is fine." He'd settled.

Fed up, Marylin did what any rational housewife in the early '70s would do when feeling neglected: She booked herself a ten-day cruise and told David to enjoy the kids. David was dumbfounded by her rashness. "This is not something married women do, running around taking cruises all by themselves," he said. "No," she clarified, walking out the door with her travel bags, "this is not something *happily* married women do, David."

The words had ten days to settle into David's heart. It was plenty of time for him to arrive at two realizations: one, running a household was just as stressful as running a business; two, if he loved Marylin—and he did—then her happiness needed to be his paramount concern. He acknowledged the need for change. "But what can I do?" he wondered. "Sure, the work schedule is killing us, but I can't just give up my business. I could probably skip the sanctuary-at-sea routine, but what's an extra hour here and there every month gonna do? And does Marylin really want to watch me defrag on the kids and her every night after my maniacal workday?"

"I've got the answer," Marylin announced after a visit with a friend. "I want you to go to a weekend marriage retreat with me," she said.

David grunted, his inner man getting uncomfortable at the very sound of "retreat." *Uh-oh, I've heard about these,* it said.

"Peggy and Dexter just got back from one and I swear they are glowing," Marylin continued. "She says it's a brand-new marriage."

Oh boy, she's getting enthusiastic—think fast! "Well, what the heck do you do there?"

"We would learn how to communicate."

"Oh . . ." *Divert, man, divert!* "But we're talking right now, aren't we?"

Marylin gave him her "not something *happily* married women do" look.

"Right," he said. "Let's look into it."

The last thing David wanted to do was take off work and go off to some weird, touchy-feely group psychotherapy session out in the middle of nowhere, but he'd decided to make changes for Marylin, and since no other alternatives for making her happy seemed available, he agreed to sign up for the weekend.

Then he devised a strategy for getting out of it.

On the Friday before the retreat weekend, David took off work—an exceptional move in and of itself—and asked Marylin if she'd like to go out on the *Sea Hunter* with him—totally unheard-of. Cruising out at sea, the two suddenly found much to talk about. For once, conversation and laughter flowed easily. "Isn't this fun?" David asked with the best puppy dog look he could muster. "Just you and me out here, having a great time together?"

Marylin smiled and nodded in agreement. "But you're still going to this retreat with me."

"What? Wait, but this is what you wanted. It seems to me we're communicating just fi—"

"Don't you dare give me that 'everything is fine' line," she cut in. "We're going."

When they arrived at the retreat that night, they were shown to their sparse, private room in a convent. The nun's bed was harder and smaller than a college dorm's. David suspected that this was either a not-so-subtle tactic to encourage physical connection, or a secret plot to keep them from sleeping at night so as to either wear them down mentally, like the military's basic training, or force them to talk more . . . or both. Lying in the tiny bed that night, "all but stacked up like a London bus" beneath Marylin, David stared at the ceiling, unable to sleep. One desperate question kept cycling through his mind: "What the hell did I get myself into?"

The next morning, that question seemed to be on every husband's mind. Marylin observed how each man held the same pose: folded arms, frowning face, apprehensive stare, clenched jaw. When the first exercise was introduced, one in which the husband and wife were instructed to write for ten minutes about their spouse's most endearing quality, a male melodrama ensued: "Ten minutes?!" "What the heck am I supposed to say to her for ten minutes?" "But I don't know how to write feelings!"

David was just as defensive as the next guy, staring at his blank notebook, trying to determine how he could write just enough to satisfy his wife without sounding like a sap. After much internal struggle, he scribbled a few things about her nice work with the kids. Her nice clothes. Swell casseroles.

Then they swapped notebooks and David read Marylin's letter to him. It was a sharp contrast to the aloof, reticent paragraph he'd just given her. It was clear that she didn't write it to impress anyone—not even him; she wrote it simply to share how she felt. It was honest. It was her. Ashamed, he looked at Marylin's eyes as she continued to read and reread his minimal effort, as if maybe a hint of deeper meaning would eventually be revealed. He saw how important this was to her. "I've emotionally estranged the woman I love," he thought.

Right then, David resolved that no matter how ridiculous and uncomfortable he felt, he would give his very best effort to share his heart, his deepest and darkest, his everything. "If Marylin really wants to know me, then I'm going to give her all of it," he decided.

Over the course of the weekend, the Geigers each discovered what made the other tick—and what made each other ticked off. Marylin learned about David's motivation to work as hard as he did, how that was what he'd been taught to do in order to be a good husband. She saw that he equated failing at work with failing her and the family, and how much he feared being a poor provider. She gained an understanding of David's stress levels and how the laundry list of parenting and house maintenance issues awaiting him at the front door every night only made the *Sea Hunter* more attractive. She decided to quit trying so hard to mold David into one of the romancing characters from the French films they used to watch.

David learned that the one time Marylin had called from the Long Island Expressway to ask him if he could take off work and come fix her flat tire—even though he'd joined AAA *specifically* for those situations—was really just a request for emotional support and sympathy. The same applied to all of the other "irritating" calls—they were simply an excuse to talk to him. He recognized how good it made Marylin feel to engage in simple heart-to-heart. He discovered that the more he shared, the more he trusted Marylin. No matter what he expressed, his weaknesses or hurt feelings, she nurtured him and respected him wholeheartedly. He realized how safe she made him feel.

At the end of the weekend, their marriage achieved a breakthrough. The final exercise was a ninety-minute writing session, with an additional ninety minutes of follow-up discussion. David's floodgates opened. He gushed onto the paper, exposing his entirety to Marylin in a way he'd never thought possible. They spent the ninety minutes of discussion time holding each other as tightly as possible, sobbing.

"It was the first time I'd ever seen him cry," Marylin says. "The things he disclosed to me during that last exercise were extremely private and personal. I felt incredibly special, honored to know him on those levels."

David laughs bashfully and shares a look of love with Marylin. "After that weekend, we did not touch the ground for a month. It was a totally transformed relationship."

"It still is today," Marylin says. "People grow and change, but not necessarily at the same time or pace and that's why we continued the daily writing and dialoguing exercises from the retreat. It's amazing what twenty minutes of one-on-one, authentic communication every day will do for a husband and wife over the course of fifty years."

"I was never as enthusiastic as Marylin about those exercises," says David. "I did them because I saw how much it improved our connection. If you have the courage to open your heart, your life together will be beautiful."

"Yep, and I have to say," Marylin says with a big smile, "lately, he's been getting so swept up in his feelings he even writes me poetry!"

David's jaw drops in disbelief, as if that was the ultimate taboo revelation. "I can't believe you just said that, babe. Now the whole world's gonna know about me!"

I'll Be Home for Christmas

Sam and Judy Smith
Married 42 years

Sam couldn't dream up a better way to spend this stormy December night. Outside, the snow was blowing sideways through the frigid Wisconsin air, while inside his beautiful wife, Judy, lounged on the living room sofa, next to Andy, his best friend since high school. Lights on the Christmas tree twinkled, Frank Sinatra's silky voice serenaded them with holiday carols, and the crackling fire promised to keep everyone warm. Andy fiddled with a deck of cards. Andy had become something of a fixture in the household lately, helping Judy to renovate their outdated kitchen and bathroom.

Looking at his two favorite people in the world, Sam thought, "Now *this* is Christmas." Noticing the empty champagne bottle, he grabbed his top-shelf vodka from the kitchen. "Shaken or stirred?" he called out in his best James Bond impression, cracking a smile.

"Uh, stirred," Andy replied.

"Judy?"

"Fine," she said.

"Stirred, then?"

"Sure, whatever."

"Where's your spirit, you two?" Sam chided as he delivered their drinks. "Let's sing, drink, and get merry!"

Sam took a candle in his free hand and sang into it like a microphone. His "Silent Night" didn't exactly harmonize with Frank's, but his performance did get Judy and Andy to crack smiles and lift their martinis.

"C'mon, Judy, you're backup," Sam coaxed, flopping next to her on the couch. "Sing with me, baby!"

Judy pushed the candle mic out of her face. "Let's just finish our card game," she suggested.

"Yeah, great idea!" Andy belted, smiling at Judy. "I'll deal."

Another round of martinis and three games later the trio had grown quiet, save for the occasional "your deal," "fold," and other necessary card banter. Judy's mind was not on the game. This was not the Christmas she'd envisioned when she and Sam married four years earlier. She'd been barely out of high school, and Sam was just a few years older, but the two had known each other since they'd played in the sandbox together in preschool. Sam had seen her through the knobby-knee phase, truly through every awkward moment of adolescence. They'd always shared hopes, dreams, and goofiness. Other couples had to adjust to one another's quirks after marriage, but not Judy and Sam. Nobody knew her, nobody understood her like her husband did.

"At least, he used to," she told herself. Sam barely had time for her anymore. She'd start telling him about her day, nothing earth-shattering, but he didn't listen. Sometimes he walked out of the room in the middle of her sentence. Their marriage wasn't awful, not like some couples'. Sam loved her. She never doubted that for a moment. But instead of bringing them closer, committing to a lifetime of togetherness had left Judy painfully lonely. Most of the time, she tried to shake off her disappointment, but all this alcohol had made her morose. Thank goodness for Andy. He actually seemed to care about the wallpaper samples she'd agonized over, and it was he, rather than her husband, who approved the new kitchen wall covering. Funny, she and Andy could talk about anything: politics, philosophy, a new recipe. He really seemed to value her opinion, the way Sam once did.

"I would like to make a toast," Sam said, "to quality time during my favorite holiday, to being with the two people I love the most: Judy, who somehow finds it in her patient soul to put up with me, and Andy, my best—and most generous—friend. Thank you for your help with the renovations."

"No problem," Andy murmured, raising his glass to Sam's.

Sam couldn't help noticing his buddy's awkward energy. "What's wrong, vodka got your tongue?" he joked, slapping Andy on the shoulder.

Andy nodded and took a deep breath. Slowly he announced, "We've been best friends for a long time, man. And there's something I . . ." He paused for a moment to glance at Judy, then looked back to his best friend. "Sam, I'm in love with your wife."

"Ha!" Sam replied. "Stop kidding around, man."

"Nothing's happened. I want you to know that. I'm not even sure she feels the same way. But I'm not kidding."

Sam's brow furrowed. He shot his wife a look, knowing she'd confirm: *This is a joke, right?*

Judy looked shocked. In all the time she had spent assisting Andy with the painting and tiling, he hadn't said one word to acknowledge his feelings. But they had definitely connected. She looked forward to his arrival every day and noticed she felt let down when other remodeling jobs kept him away. Perhaps this was what fate had intended all along. Much to her surprise, Judy found herself saying, "I think I've fallen in love with him, too."

Sam's stomach dropped. He stared into her guilty eyes. A series of images flashed furiously through his mind: the sandbox, playing kick the can as kids, driving up to Lovers' Point, where they kissed for hours, Judy walking down the aisle of the old country church on their wedding day, their very first Christmas with their makeshift tree in their tiny apartment. Then his mind snapped to the images of his best man, Andy, congratulating him, congratulating Judy; his generous friend, Andy, hugging Judy to celebrate the last coat of paint in the upstairs bathroom; his true friend, Andy, sitting in the kitchen, talking to Judy until the wee hours of the night while she waited for her husband finally to come home from work.

Filled with rage, Sam began ripping ornaments from the tree. Then he grabbed his jacket and car keys and stormed out the front door into the blizzard. Driving through his neighborhood, he couldn't see more than a foot ahead of him, but he didn't care. His entire future had become a great, blinding unknown.

"How did this happen?" Sam kept asking himself. He and Judy were happy. That is, they had been. Lately, he'd found himself regretting that they'd married so young. He longed for the excitement and freedom his buddies enjoyed. He felt tied down by marriage. So he'd join the guys for the occasional beer or poker game after work. Soon he found himself arranging his schedule so that nothing interfered with buddy time. No curfew for them; why did Sam need one? He'd come home late to find Judy in bed and a beautifully arranged plate of food in the fridge, covered in tin foil. He started to remember all the times he'd plopped himself in front of the television, tuning out Judy when she tried to talk to him. Sam shook his head, thinking how he brushed off Judy's multiple attempts to engage him in the house renovation, telling her he was "way too busy for that decorating stuff" and to "call Andy, he doesn't have anything better to do."

The sun was just peeking above the white, tree-lined horizon when Sam finally pulled back into his driveway. He was relieved to see Andy's car gone but dreaded facing his wife. The longer he sat in the car, the more his fear mounted. Fear pushed his defensive buttons: *So you're not going to win any Husband of the Year awards—big deal. She betrayed you, Sam! She's the one who ought to be begging for forgiveness! Stand up for yourself, man.*

Sam's head dropped and he began to weep. The realization that he had chosen his drinking buddies over his own wife sickened him. The thought of losing Judy made his whole body ache. He made a decision: *I have to take responsibility for this.* Sam recognized that he was the one who had allowed the marriage to wither. He couldn't remember the last time they had talked about something other than his work or whether to buy a new lawn mower. In that moment he resolved to fight for his marriage.

When Sam entered the house, Judy was sitting at the kitchen table, resting her head in her hands. Sam pulled out a chair across from her.

"I'm sorry," he said, sitting down.

Sam's apology took Judy off guard. "Why are you apologizing to me?" she asked.

"Because I caused this. I haven't loved you the way you deserve."

He took her hands in his. "I haven't been a good husband and I know that. But I'm asking you for one thing."

"What?" whispered Judy.

"I'm asking you for one month. Give me thirty days to prove my love to you. If at the end of the month you want to go with him, I won't try to stop you."

"All right, thirty days," replied Judy.

Every night after work Sam drove straight home. He and Judy sat at the kitchen table, long after dinner was finished. They talked, sometimes for five hours at a stretch. Sam was completely honest. He acknowledged his longing for freedom but assured his wife that that feeling had passed. "I thought my friends had something I didn't," he told her. "Turns out it was the other way around."

By the end of the week, Judy had made up her mind. She tried to explain her declaration about Andy. "I was so lonely. You were gone all the time. And I missed how we used to talk about everything together. I wanted to do more than just get by. I think I just got confused. I wasn't in love with Andy. I just wanted to be loved again." Tears began to stream down her cheeks. "I'm so sorry."

Sam held her tightly. "Me too," he whispered. "We're in this marriage together. For life."

Today, forty-two years into their marriage, it's obvious that Sam had meant what he said. Their low point is a distant memory and their connection is truly vibrant.

"It's easy to look for greener pastures once the initial bloom of love is gone. You lose faith," Judy says, sitting in the family room of their Wisconsin home. "But don't wait for a new Prince Charming to fill that void before you tell your mate how you're feeling about the marriage. The love you're missing isn't as far away as you think."

"I agree," says Sam. "And be careful not to fall into the trap of neglecting your spouse, particularly in the early stages of a marriage. If you find yourselves drifting apart, take responsibility for your actions, put your ego aside, and be the husband you promised to be. The only person you can truly change is yourself."

Judy looks proudly at the man she'd met in a sandbox, acknowledging their relationship's growth. "I couldn't ask for a more deep and meaningful connection than the one I have with Sam."

Sam likes what he hears. "See? This is proof that there's hope for us clueless men."

Always the Student
Perry and Carolyn Ehrenstein
Married 54 years

Carolyn sits at her husband's bedside and confides her greatest fear: "I don't know what I'm going to do when you're gone," she tells him. "I can't imagine my life without you." Perry doesn't answer. Often, he lacks the strength to talk. But words aren't always needed now, because husband and wife understand each other so well. In this marriage of fifty-four years, every feeling is shared. No worry or fear or shame is held back. And no expression of love has gone unspoken.

"We've had a great marriage," says Carolyn. "If we hadn't learned to communicate the way we do, I don't know how we could go through what we're going through."

Perry's heart had been faltering for years. Surgery after surgery, he always managed to bounce back. "Even in the hospital, he'd tell jokes and make me laugh," Carolyn says. Then Perry was diagnosed with lymphoma, and bouncing back no longer seemed likely. The couple faced a difficult decision: buy time with chemotherapy and its potentially brutal side effects, or forgo treatment. "We disagreed at first. Then we talked and talked about every part of this. In the end, we wanted the same thing," she says.

The couple didn't always communicate so openly. Never mind life-and-death issues—for years, Perry didn't even share his feelings about what car to buy. As a result, the couple would trade in their two-door for another two-door, while Perry secretly yearned to drive off the lot in the latest four-door model. To Perry's way of thinking, peace-keeping, not communicating, made a marriage work. And his was working just fine, he thought, until his wife told him otherwise. . . .

In a quarter century of marriage, Perry and Carolyn never fought and rarely bickered. There were no slammed doors, hurled insults, or veiled threats in the Ehrenstein household. So when Carolyn suggested they attend a workshop to improve their communication, Perry balked. "I don't feel the need to bare my soul to strangers," he told her. "If you need to learn to communicate better, why don't you go?"

Carolyn sighed. With the kids grown and gone, she often felt stumped for meaningful conversation with her husband. Once a week, they scheduled a "date," a dinner for the two of them to relax and get caught up: Perry would talk about his YMCA board meeting, and Carolyn, the latest staff changes at the medical supply company where she worked in accounting. Then they'd wash the dishes and race off to their respective meetings. Somehow, these brief information exchanges didn't bring the closeness Carolyn sought. As much as she loved her husband, she was lonely. "There's got to be more to marriage than this," Carolyn thought.

Ever the peacemaker, Perry reluctantly agreed to attend the workshop, all the while thinking, "I don't think I need to know her feelings, and she doesn't need to know mine." But something in the material resonated with Perry, and when it came his turn to share, he said more about himself in twenty-five seconds than Carolyn had heard in twenty-five years. The program leaders were so moved by Perry and Carolyn, they encouraged the couple to become leaders themselves and assist other couples.

Over the next several years, their marriage blossomed. For the first time, Perry, who'd once prided himself on "staying out of arguments like crazy," allowed himself a contrary opinion now and then. He recognized his feelings were "neither right nor wrong," and also that his marriage wouldn't crumble if he and his wife held contrary views on which automobile to purchase. Both became better listeners, paying attention to what the other had to say, instead of tuning out while composing a reply.

Not only did they become leaders in the faith-based "Marriage Encounter," they were among the program's most popular teachers. Newly bonded couples credited Perry and Carolyn for turning their relationship around. They showered the Ehrensteins with praise. The couple received so many letters of gratitude they bought a special box just to store them all.

But their level of involvement took its toll on Carolyn. Meetings and more meetings, brainstorming sessions, and weekend-long workshops on top of her full-time job left Carolyn exhausted. When her brother died unexpectedly of a heart attack, she felt utterly overwhelmed. When it was time to lead the next discussion on the schedule—coping with the death of a loved one—Carolyn knew she just wasn't up to it.

She finally told Perry, "There's no way I can do this anymore. I'm getting out. You can stay in if you want."

Only couples assumed positions of leadership. Carolyn knew the rules as well as her husband. That meant Perry was out, too.

Never had Perry known such adulation as he received from those young couples in Marriage Encounter. Nothing in his ordinary life had ever made him feel this special and important. "It's amazing how they look up to me," he thought. It's not that his family didn't love and appreciate him. They did. Others valued Perry, too, as a volunteer board member, and at the clothing business where he worked as a production manager.

But Marriage Encounter had made him a star. All the attention and praise heaped on Perry made him feel like a pastor or a famous speaker. Young men looked at Perry as the model of a husband they might one day become. The glory surpassed even the fleeting sports triumphs of his youth. "That was here today and gone tomorrow," he thought, "but this stays with you." In fact, Perry's role in Marriage Encounter had become as much a part of his identity as his career.

Thanks to Carolyn, he could kiss all that adulation good-bye. "How could you?" he thought. "How could you take this away from me?"

Aloud, he said only one word: "Fine."

Marriage Encounter had taught him he should express his feelings openly and honestly, knowing he would not be judged. But Perry kept silent. After all, Carolyn's decision was "a done deal," he thought. The whole topic felt dangerous to him, and Perry preferred sharing only safe feelings. Best just to forget the whole thing, he told himself. He and Carolyn had worked hard to build a great relationship, why take risks now?

Indeed, the Ehrensteins continued to manage just fine, with one exception: Perry's hands. The arthritis he'd coped with for some time became far worse, gnarling his fingers. Often he could not close his hands at all. For six years, nothing the doctor prescribed helped, and Perry's only relief came from plunging his hands in ice water.

Then one weekend, while Carolyn was out of town, Perry attended a seminar at their church. A visiting pastor was speaking on the link between physical and emotional healing.

The first day, the pastor took one look at Perry's hands and asked if his marriage was troubled.

"My marriage is fine," Perry told him.

The second day, the pastor announced to the congregation, "There's a middle-aged man here with arthritis who hasn't forgiven his wife."

"Now wait a minute . . ." Perry began. Then he looked at his hands and for the first time saw in his clenched fingers the resentment he'd been holding onto so tightly. Hurt, anger, and betrayal rose to the surface like bile, and Perry felt himself mentally vomit those long-harbored feelings out of his system. His heart told him what he'd been communicating to Carolyn without words:

I'll never forgive you for this. In that moment of recognition, his hands began to heal.

And Perry and Carolyn went back to work on their marriage. All this time, Carolyn had no inkling of her husband's resentment. Perry had thought that he and wife had already grown as close as two people could and feared jeopardizing that relationship. They both discovered how much more they had to learn about each other. Perry began sharing all his feelings, not just the safe ones. They both allowed themselves to be vulnerable with each other. The fruit of their labor was a closeness neither had imagined. "A great marriage isn't something you make happen once," Carolyn realized. "You have to keep nurturing it to keep the love flowing."

Open communication has distinguished their marriage ever since, even more so since Perry was diagnosed with cancer. "We can say freely whatever is on our minds and know the response is welcome," Carolyn says. Perry doesn't have to pretend he's fine when he's feeling lousy. Carolyn can tell her husband how she dreads being alone. After much heartfelt discussion, the couple agreed to stop Perry's chemotherapy treatments. Carolyn says they're at peace with the decision.

"So many people die full of regret," she says, "wishing they'd been closer to their husband or wife. They're sorry for not having said 'I love you' more often." In the Ehrenstein marriage, there are no regrets. At one time, young couples' adulation made Perry feel special and important. In the end, the admiration of others paled in comparison to the greatness he found in the relationship with his wife.

Chapter 6

What's the Number One Secret to an Amazing Marriage?

PERFECT STRANGERS

— by Mat

Arm in arm, the seventy-something couple stood on the front porch of their suburban Cleveland home and waved good-bye to us. But behind the smiles and best wishes for a safe journey, I could see the wife's expression was slightly troubled, and that the husband was shaking his head. Jason and I had spent the last few hours asking this couple about their number one secret to an amazing marriage, and we left with full notebooks and videotapes and pockets stuffed with homemade cookies. These Marriage Masters had shared generously with us—both their lives and baked goods. I don't think for a minute they regretted their candor. No, it wasn't their relationship that concerned them.

It was ours: Jason's and mine.

We'd arrived cheerful and joking, but it was all an act. The tension between my best friend and me was impossible to hide for long. When the wife asked Jason why a handsome and charming young man like him wasn't taken, I couldn't resist blurting out, "It's his gas problems!" Nobody laughed, especially not Jason, who feigned a "wasn't that just hilarious" look. But he'd already gone out of his way to piss me off that morning, insisting we stop at the corner minimart for sunflower seeds when we were already running late for the interview. He knows I hate to be late. By contrast, a day without someone waiting on Jason is a day wasted in his mind. Or so it seemed.

Six weeks into our cross-country journey—interviewing Marriage Masters to find out what made relationships last—Jason and I still had three more weeks to go. Quite frankly, I doubted we'd last that long. We'd had some blowouts before, but they'd always blown over. Certainly, two best friends, crammed in a small space for a long period of time, would grow irritated with each other. But our relationship had left irritation behind nine states back. Now it was more like a thousand Freddy Krueger knife fingers scratching a giant chalkboard. Until we'd committed to this level of togetherness, I'd never realized quite how much Jason's tardiness disturbed me. That, and everything else.

Like those sunflower seeds! Jason liked to eat them in the RV. With bulging cheeks similar to a chipmunk's crammed with seeds, he'd spit the saliva-covered shells in an empty coffee cup, filling it to the brim. When we took corners, the cup would spill, dumping slimy shells on the carpet. Jason would casually scoop them up with his hand, missing at least half. I asked him repeatedly not to leave his shells in the cup, to no avail. I had also asked him nicely not to flush them down the RV toilet, because of the clogging factor. He never listened. I was sick and tired of cleaning up after him. After a while, the very sound of his mouth blowing seeds into the cup made me want to pull over and toss Jason out on the side of the road. He might as well have been spitting those seeds at me.

By the time we'd pulled up to our Marriage Masters' house that morning, I thought, "That's it. Let's call off the friendship right now." The thought of twenty-three more seed-blowing, late-starting, Jason-filled days was unbearable. I consoled myself that once we got home, he could go his way and I would go mine. But I also couldn't help but wonder: What had gone wrong? We used to be so close, like brothers even. What ingredient had disappeared from a relationship that been going strong since third grade?

Although I was slow to comprehend, the answer came during our interview in Cleveland that day. Actually, we'd heard the same answer in an earlier interview, the day before. And the interview before that. And in several dozen more as we zigzagged thousands of miles from LA to Cleveland. It didn't matter where the couples lived, how long they'd been married, or the balance in their bank account. As we listened to couples talk about the number one secret to an amazing marriage, it became clear from their unanimous answers that the secret to marital success is respect.

Respect? The Holy Grail of marriage is respect? Umm, yeah . . . Is there anything else in that magic marital bag of secrets you've got?

"What a letdown," I always thought. It seemed to me that respect was a given in marriage, like an exchange of rings at the altar. Respect was . . . not exactly boring, but pretty basic. As a kid, think of everyone you're taught to respect: parents, elders, teachers, the police officer on the corner. Surely, respecting your spouse—the person you want to spend your life with—this should be a piece of cake, right? If all you had to do was respect your partner, why did so many people get divorced?

The troubled gaze of our Marriage Masters seemed to follow me through suburban Cleveland that morning, until it finally hit me: The ingredient missing from the relationship between Jason and me *was* respect. At some level, I think I already knew that. I knew I'd treated him disrespectfully, but I just couldn't stop myself. As we headed to our next interview, the angst churned my stomach, making me slightly nauseous.

No sooner did we find the house than my cell phone rang. The wife of the couple we were interviewing told us they had to run out and would be back home in twenty minutes. I turned off the motor. Jason leaned his head back on the seat, turned away from me, and closed his eyes. He can endure long awkward silences with ease. For me, the curtain of stillness that hung between us made the RV claustrophobic, so I busied myself trying to pinpoint the moment our relationship had begun to unravel. I realized there was no one moment, no one situation big enough to merit my distaste for his very presence. Instead, there was an accumulating pattern of events. Certainly his constant tardiness felt contemptuous, because he knows how much I hate being late. But it was more than that. Take the Marriage Masters we were about to interview. I didn't get mad at them for not being ready on time. I wasn't going to roll my eyes, huff, puff, or turn my back on them. But Jason, on the other hand, would get a full helping of all the above if he scampered down to the RV five minutes late—and he's supposed to be my best friend, for God's sake.

It was with immense resistance that I realized that, like most simple answers, the complexity didn't lie in the mind but in the will. I knew what respect meant—honoring and valuing another person. I just couldn't seem to practice it with my best friend. In recent weeks, I showed complete strangers more courtesy than I did Jason. I took satisfaction over challenging his every decision, cutting him off midsentence, capitalizing on opportunities to belittle him in front of people. Our formerly teasing banter had vanished. We no longer poked fun at each other but jabbed painfully. Imagine if we'd pledged not just a few weeks, but a lifetime in this RV. We'd go nuts! One of us would surely bail.

"Is this how it all begins?" I wondered. "Is this, what's happening to our friendship, what turns a good marriage bad?" Two people committed to travel through life together veer off down a bumpy road and never find their way back to the highway (with the man, of course, refusing to stop and ask for directions). One irritation doesn't break a relationship, but take that one annoyance, respond to it with defensiveness, fling back some sarcasm, turn away with seething resentment that boils over into rage, seek opportunities to publicly humiliate and belittle, tally your victories, twist an innocent comment so that "Let's stay home for dinner" is translated as "You're too cheap to take me out," and pretty soon the only sounds coming from your dinner table are the clattering of flatware and chewing of food.

Disrespect can become a pattern of behavior that's difficult to break. I knew that I had been treating Jason disrespectfully. I wanted to stop, but it was as if our cycle of disrespect had its own gravitational pull. Even though my head knew it was wrong, my emotions would get the best of me and my knee-jerk reaction to any imagined slight was criticism or defensiveness. Then he'd fire back and I'd feel temporary satisfaction that I'd wounded him. Apparently, it's easier to listen to 250 hours of couples discussing respect than to actually practice it for three days straight. After all, Jason and I were about to "divorce" a twenty-plus-year friendship over sunflower seeds.

I realized then what the Marriage Masters had been trying to tell us. You have to be vigilant about honing this discipline. It was like a muscle they had built up over the years and, when compared to mine, it was like Schwarzenegger's quadriceps next to a drumstick. Don't get me wrong, the Marriage Masters treated their spouses disrespectfully at times, too. But whether it was a single incident or an emerging pattern, they not only recognized what was happening, they did something about it. They allowed each other to grow and change. They listened when they'd have rather tuned out. And each stood up for the other, even at the expense of their own comfort. This newfound and deepened respect became the pattern that defined their relationship over decades to come.

Maybe the number one secret to a successful marriage wasn't so simple after all.

When it was time for our next interview, Jason and I hopped out of the RV, rang the doorbell, and faked really big smiles.

"Man, you guys are rollin' in style," the couple said, looking out at the RV. "How long have you been on the road?"

Jason and I both took deep breaths. "Oh, about six weeks."

"So are you guys ready to kill each other yet?" They laughed.

We didn't answer. Instead, we followed them inside to a cozy living room, and let everyone get comfortable.

Then Jason turned on the video camera and I asked the big question, "So what's *your* secret to staying married for fifty years?"

War on the Home Front

Jack and Dorothy Manin
Married 63 years

Stationed eighteen months in Japan during the Korean War, Jack Manin longed for home. He had spent nearly a third of his marriage overseas, first on a navy minesweeper during World War II, and now as a third-class engineman helping to rebuild the country he'd once been ordered to invade. Jack trained Japanese workers to become mechanics. He learned their language, befriending many of his new coworkers. But the pace was grueling, and the atmosphere tense. No one spoke of Hiroshima or Nagasaki, of atomic mushroom clouds rising miles in the air, and especially of the more than two hundred thousand Japanese wiped out by the blasts and their aftermath. They did talk about the threat of the Korean conflict spreading to Japan, that war could break out there any moment. Jack had vowed to serve his country, no questions asked, but he had no desire to see battle, not ever again.

Visions of home had sustained Jack through his time at sea during the last war. He would imagine Dorothy, his bride of four years, and his baby daughter. He loved to replay the night he met his future wife. Jack couldn't believe he'd almost passed up the blind date. At a dance in a small country grange, he and Dorothy danced and talked as if they'd known each other for years. She looked gorgeous in her black taffeta dress with white petticoat.

"I don't plan to be a housewife," Dorothy told him. "I'm going to work in an office, maybe run it someday." Jack had never met a girl so forward thinking.

When they attempted a jazzy swing dance called the Big Apple, Dorothy swung so hard the buttons popped off her dress. An embarrassed Dorothy stood there, holding her dress together, as Jack risked his fingers among the stomping shoes to retrieve the buttons that had scattered all over the dance floor. She thanked him for being a gentleman, then hightailed it to the rest room for a quick dress repair. Driving home that night, there was no doubt in his mind he had met his "best girl."

After World War II, Jack settled into life at home. Baby Mary was only five months old when war took him away again. Jack knew how lonely Dorothy had been the last time he left. "This time, I'm going to take better care of her while I'm gone," he thought. He hatched a brilliant plan, keeping it a secret until just before he shipped out.

"Guess what! I asked Mom and Pop to move in and keep you company while I'm gone. Isn't that great?"

He could still see the look of stunned surprise on Dorothy's face when he broke the news. "Wow! She must really be touched," Jack thought. Dorothy's lips moved but no words came out. She looked like she was about to cry.

There on the ship, he would close his eyes and try to imagine everyone at home—Dorothy and his mom, Evelyn, cooking spaghetti together, laughing as his dad, John, and older daughter, Jackie, begged for a taste. No barking orders, no rumbling

engines, no fear that war could erupt at any moment and chaos ensue.

When the orders came ending his tour of duty, Jack couldn't wait to head home. He'd already spent too much of his married life in battle or mopping up after it. Jack boarded a transport ship bound for Seattle, imagining the joyful reunion with his family.

"Where were you?" Dorothy's father-in-law demanded. "Out runnin' around with some other guy?"

Dorothy, arms full of groceries, strode quickly to the kitchen. "They needed me to stay late at the office again," she told John, trying to remain cordial.

"I just bet."

Dorothy slammed cans of peas into the cupboard. She clanked and stacked the dinner dishes and yanked open the drawer of silver to set the table. Dorothy transcribed business correspondence at Viewmaster, a company that manufactured a device for viewing 3-D images. She was proud to contribute to household expenses. She labored forty hours a week elbow to elbow in a noisy room packed with typists, and her father-in-law acted like she spent her days gallivanting around like some floozy.

The house had only one bedroom, which Jack's parents had claimed. This left Dorothy, daughter Jackie, seven, baby Mary, and Jack's little sister to share the unfinished attic. John appointed himself "man of the house" in Dorothy's house. The cramped space could barely contain all the extra bodies, let alone John's rules. John decided what radio program the family would hear each night and even what time dinner would be served. The fact that Dorothy worked every day in an office made his blood boil.

"You should be doing a woman's work in the kitchen, not out there in a man's world," he told her each morning.

"Good-bye, John," she'd say and head out the front door.

"Your skirt's too tight!" he'd yell after her.

How she longed to tell this surly ingrate to go home! She also longed to tell her husband. But she could do neither. Like other women, Dorothy had been raised not to talk back to her elders. And Jack? How could she upset Jack when he was thousands of miles away? He'd been so proud; she couldn't bear for her beloved husband to know that his "gift" was ruining her life. Around Jack, John had always been polite to Dorothy. So she bit her lip and said nothing. "Things are just great here at home," she wrote to Jack.

The night before Jack's return, Dorothy was too excited to sleep. She could think of nothing but holding her husband tight, kissing his handsome face, and stacking her in-laws' luggage on the sidewalk.

No sooner was Jack off the ship than Dorothy threw her arms around him and gave him the kiss she'd been saving up for a year and a half. "I'm not going to spoil this," she told herself. "I won't say a word about his dad."

Dorothy's resolve lasted about ten minutes. The drive from Seattle to Portland lasted four hours.

"Honey, don't you worry," he assured her. "I'm back now. Mom and Pop will want to go back to their own place."

One week later, the only change to the cramped household was the addition of Jack. To Dorothy's dismay, Jack avoided asking his parents to leave. "Tell them we need our privacy," Dorothy prodded.

Jack didn't know what to say. He'd fantasized a peaceful sanctuary only to enter a cold war. His father expected Dorothy to be a servant, a "good little wife," who never crossed the boundary into a "man's world." "I'm sure he didn't mean it that way," Jack would tell himself after one of John's subtle slights. His bubbly, vivacious wife alternately slumped and seethed. Jack just wanted everyone to get along. He wanted to be soothed by happy, homey chatter. Suddenly being in Japan with the threat of hostility from Korea offered more refuge than his own living room.

One night over dinner, John casually said, "Since we are going to be living here a while, Jack, you and I should think about fixing some of my old cars."

Dorothy almost choked on her meat loaf.

Jack swallowed hard, trying to ease the tension in his gut. "Yup," he squeaked.

Dorothy smacked Jack's knee under the table. He clenched his teeth and pursed his lips at her as if to say, "Back off!" But she met him eye to eye, equally intense, her expression saying, "I have been, buster, but no more!"

Later that night, the couple once again stared up at the attic rafters, their daughters crammed in a single bed next to them, Jack's sister on a mattress next to them. For the first time in their marriage, Dorothy felt betrayed. For a year and a half, she'd waited for the day he would come home and make everything better. His inaction had only made things worse. "Why can't he be in my corner?" she wondered.

"I married you, Jack," Dorothy said. "Not your mom and dad."

Jack couldn't bear the sadness and disappointment in her voice. He tossed and turned for hours. What could he do? Tell the father who raised him and sacrificed for him that he was no longer welcome? "Maybe Dad will come around and respect that Dorothy really wants to work," he told himself. Better yet, maybe his dad would choose to move out on his own. Wouldn't that be great! "It could still happen," Jack assured himself.

After three and a half years of war, what Jack wanted most in his life was peace. Now he wondered if the price was too high. Jack realized he valued his wife's happiness far more.

The next morning, Jack entered the kitchen and kissed Dorothy, who was finishing a cup of tea before leaving for work. John sat at the table, devouring the breakfast Evelyn had cooked for him. He beckoned Jack to his ear and stage-whispered loud enough for Dorothy to hear, "Son, doesn't your own wife know you can support her? I don't understand why she thinks she belongs in a man's world."

Dorothy gave Jack a piercing look, ready to take scalps. Jack willed the butterflies in his stomach to stop flapping their wings. What he valued above all else was Dorothy. But by allowing Pop to treat her like this, he himself was not respecting his wife.

"Pop, you can't say that about my wife. I love that Dorothy wants to work."

"So now you're hiding behind a skirt? What's that woman done to you, boy?"

"You know what?" Jack said. "Maybe you and Mom would be happier if you found a place of your own."

John slowly wiped his mouth with his napkin. He didn't even look at Jack when he said, "So we're too big a burden?"

"No, not at all," Jack said, backpedaling. "It's just that my wife and my girls and I are our own family now and we need our space."

Dorothy and Evelyn stood transfixed, waiting for the volcano to erupt.

"So this is how you repay us after all we've done for you," John said gravely. "By kicking us out?"

This time, Jack would not back down. "You don't have to look at it that way. You and Mom will be happier with your own place, and so will we."

"Fine!" John shouted, throwing down his napkin. "C'mon, Evelyn, let's get outta their hair!"

John and Evelyn retreated to the bedroom to pack. Jack exhaled, hoping some of his tension would escape. Dorothy gently wrapped him in her arms. The warm kiss on his cheek reassured him that he had done the right thing.

For the next month, John refused Jack's calls, but finally father and son reunited. Never again did John criticize Dorothy for working, and the two eventually became friends. Space would heal their injured relationship.

But the biggest shift took place between Dorothy and Jack. He'd always respected Dorothy. He was fond of saying he admired her more than anyone else in the world. Now he realized that to honor one's wife was not an abstract concept put forth in a wedding vow. He needed to actively demonstrate his respect. That meant no one could criticize Dorothy, and he and his wife would refrain from criticizing each other in front of oth-

ers. If he thought she'd been too strict with the kids, he waited until they were alone, and even then began "What do you think about . . . ?" or "I have a suggestion . . ." instead of "How could you?" Dorothy found her own respect deepening. She enthusiastically attended social functions that didn't interest her except that they were important to Jack. And if Dorothy was sad or down, Jack didn't automatically try to cheer her up. He showed consideration for how she was feeling. Mutual respect became the hallmark of a loving marriage that spanned sixty-three years.

Dorothy squeezed Jack's hand and remembered a prayer that had always guided her toward respect in marriage: "Make me easy, Lord I pray, easy to live with throughout each day."

Shortly before Jack passed away, he was asked, "What's been your greatest success in life?" Without hesitation, he answered, "My relationship with Dorothy."

> ## *Domestic Disturbance*
> ### Don and Barbara Morris
> ### Married 60 years

One bright Sunday morning in the spring of 1971, Barbara Morris had an epiphany. She was sitting in church, trying not to doze as the pastor droned on about "sinners in hell," when all of a sudden she realized she didn't like what she was hearing.

She sat up straighter in the uncomfortable pew and really listened to the sermon the pastor was spewing from the pulpit. And each time he mentioned hell, Barbara was surprised to find herself shuddering. Everything the pastor said just sounded *wrong*.

Something inside Barbara told her no such place existed. Surely a God who loved all his creations wouldn't punish them for their mistakes with eternal hellfire.

Although Barbara attended church regularly, she realized she had never truly contemplated exactly what her beliefs were. And while she didn't have a ready answer, there was one thing she was sure of: She couldn't believe in a God like the one the pastor was describing.

So she decided right then and there to find a God she could believe in.

"Maybe God's a woman," Barbara remarked to Don, her husband of twenty years.

Don rolled his eyes, flicking on the turn signal and moving the car into the left lane.

He didn't know what had gotten into Barbara lately. She was acting like a different person. Someone flaky and cuckoo, not the logical, pragmatic woman he had married.

He missed that woman.

Don and Barbara were both geologists. They'd always approached life the same way they approached the specimens they found embedded in the earth: sensibly, scientifically, and with a healthy dose of skepticism. They couldn't pick up a chunk of rock without pondering its physical and chemical properties and categorizing it as igneous, sedimentary, or metamorphic. But no longer.

Ever since that day in church, Barbara had been on a quest to figure out exactly where her beliefs lay. She began to formulate her ideas of God and the divine by looking within, by asking herself what kind of God she *felt* existed.

Studying different religious texts and philosophies made her realize that her life needed a greater spiritual element. The new books she was reading led her to meetings of different spiritual groups, like the one she and Don had just attended.

The people she met at her groups believed in a God that didn't judge. Unfortunately, the same couldn't be said about her husband.

"What was with all that chanting nonsense?" Don asked, steering past the car next to them, then moving back into the right lane. He'd finally agreed to accompany Barbara to one of her meetings and was left more bewildered than ever about this new side to his wife.

"They're feeling the spirit of God within themselves," answered Barbara.

"They *think* they're feeling the spirit. You and I know they're not."

"I believe they are. It's an inner experience that can't be put into words—"

"Nor can it be proved. The whole thing is just silly," he said, glancing over at his wife. "I hope you're not going to *that* group again."

"I enjoy the group. You don't have to go, but you can't stop me from going."

Don rolled his eyes again, letting out a frustrated breath.

To Don, the whole thing was pretty far-fetched. How did his wife know just by feeling that something was true? As a geologist, Don couldn't respect truths gained through intuition. He didn't clutch rocks in his hands and hope they revealed climate conditions from thousands of years ago; he broke them apart and systematically studied them.

Since Barbara was a geologist too, it didn't make sense that she would allow her emotions so much power. Science was all about being objective, Don thought, to better capture the true nature of the world. The people in Galileo's time had *felt* that Earth was flat, but they had been wrong; their senses had deceived them. Don wondered if his wife was letting her senses deceive her.

In any case, he was tired of talking about it. Better just to keep his mouth shut and concentrate on driving them home.

Don and Barbara had met at the University of Iowa, while they were both working toward their master's degrees. They began dating, and when they finished school and Barbara got a job teaching at Augustana College in Rock Island, Illinois, Don drove up every weekend from Iowa. When they got married, both agreed they wanted a traditional marriage, one that was 'til death do them part. If disagreements came up, they would be worked through.

Since Don and Barbara were so much alike, both geologists, both with traditional religious backgrounds—him Lutheran, her Methodist—they assumed that their common interests and love for each other would sustain their marriage. And they did.

Of course, they seldom talked about religion.

A few days after going to the meeting with Don, Barbara had what she felt was a total experience of knowing. She had spent the day in bed meditating and searching within herself for the inner truth she believed would answer her questions, and after hours and hours of deep thought, she felt a wave of love wash over her. Not just romantic or familial love, but a deep, unconditional love that was a part of everything. Though she couldn't explain it in words, the feeling she felt was so powerful that she knew it was a sign that she'd discovered her truth. It was *God*.

High on her revelation, Barbara left the bedroom and found Don in the living room reading. She told him about what she had found searching deep inside her own spirit. "It's a deep feeling of love I get from the universe."

"I don't want to hear about it," said Don, not lifting his eyes from his book.

"I need you to respect my feelings," said Barbara.

"I don't think they deserve respect. I think you're starting to sound a little nuts."

Barbara walked out of the room, and Don stared unhappily at his book, not seeing any of the words printed there. He hated all the fighting, but he didn't know what to say to Barbara anymore. Don felt excluded from Barbara's spiritual experiences, but he wasn't comfortable pretending to believe in them just for the sake of making things more comfortable.

Barbara was also angry. Don kept belittling her beliefs. By showing a lack of respect for her spiritual journey, he was showing a lack of respect for her. It especially bothered her when he cut her off every time she mentioned something spiritual. How could she stay with a man who belittled what was most important to her?

Finally, frustrated with Don's unwillingness to respect her beliefs, Barbara told him they were through, and the two separated. She still loved Don, but she felt in her heart that they couldn't stay together under the circumstances.

Don moved out of the house into an apartment but soon found himself at loose ends and filled with regret. While he was skeptical of Barbara's new modernized spirituality, he didn't want it to be the thing that ended their marriage. He was still in love with her, regardless of her spiritual beliefs. And after four months apart, Don realized he couldn't live without her.

He knew that the only way to win his wife back was to show her that he respected her newfound spirituality. So he sought out the books he'd seen on Barbara's nightstand. And while the books still didn't appeal to his scientific sense of the world, reading them was the only way he could think to connect with the woman he wasn't sure he knew anymore.

Don and Barbara both wanted to reconcile, but they knew that if they did, it had to be with the understanding that respect had to be the cornerstone of their relationship. Whatever they thought about each other's beliefs, it was important that they respected the other person's right to believe.

They both began to understand that the strength of their relationship was more important than their individual beliefs. To get back together, they needed to find a common ground, a space to discuss what they believed without feeling judged or ridiculed. Respect didn't have to mean agreeing with everything the other person believed, only attempting to understand and respect those beliefs because they were held by someone you loved dearly.

One night, Don called the house. "It's me," he said when Barbara answered the phone. "I've been reading some of those books you like. . . ."

Barbara took a deep breath. As grateful as she was that he was reading the texts that were so important to her, she was afraid that he would dismiss them as nonsense. "And?" she asked tentatively.

"And I'm trying to think about what they're saying. It's hard, but I'm trying."

A relieved smile spread across Barbara's face. "That's good."

"I'd like it a lot if we could talk about them," Don said. "Maybe . . . maybe there's something in them for me, something I can connect with."

"We can do that. I'd like that a lot."

"I think . . . I think I was far too flippant about the books and your groups and I'm sorry. It's just . . . All this stuff sounds so strange to me, like God being a woman—"

"God's not necessarily a woman. It's up to each of us to look inside ourselves and decide what God is."

There was a long pause. "I think maybe I'm ready to do that," said Don.

A week later, Don moved back into the house, and he and Barbara have stayed together ever since. It hasn't always been easy—Don still doesn't entirely understand his wife's spiritual life. He does his best, though, asking questions and reading books, and most of all listening to her when she talks about it, regardless of how uncomfortable or alienated it makes him feel. "Allowing your partner to be an individual—which means sometimes holding opposing core beliefs—takes great strength, especially when it comes to religion," he says. "But as long as you respect each other, having different beliefs won't reduce the amount of love in your marriage."

Barbara also keeps in mind how difficult it is for Don to understand her beliefs and appreciates the fact that he is trying at all. "Don may never come to fully agree with what it is that I believe to be true, and that's okay."

Because what Don and Barbara both realized is that, regardless of their specific individual religious beliefs, when they look into their hearts, they both feel love bursting inside them . . . love for each other.

And that is the only truth they need.

Mute Point

Terry and Louie Santa Maria
Married 55 years

It had been a year to remember for most folks. The Suez Canal was reopened in the spring. Jimmy Hoffa was arrested for bribery. The Dodgers swapped Brooklyn for Los Angeles. And arguably the most important development: The Wham-O company gave the world a plastic flying thing called a Frisbee.

But for diehard USC Trojans football fans like Louie Santa Maria, it had been a year to immediately forget. Going into the season finale with a dismal one and eight record, including an excruciating loss to the baby blues across town, and not a sliver of hope for a bowl game, only one thing could possibly salvage the year for the cardinal red and gold faithful: a W against the Fightin' Irish of Notre Dame.

Saturday morning, November 30, 1957, Louie woke up chanting, "Fight on for Ol' SC."

It was a sweet distraction for Louie, a man whose life otherwise revolved around providing his wife, Terry, his four children, and his elderly mother with food and shelter. Love in the household was always aplenty; the same could not be said for money. Despite working two jobs from 7 A.M. to 10 P.M. daily and even most weekends, Louie rarely had enough cash to pay the utility bills at month's end, not even with the monthly check from the U.S. government—its way of saying, "Sorry, and thanks for taking one for the team," for his service in the Army Air Corps, from which he was medically discharged after his four years of crewing fighter planes left him legally deaf.

But today he was free from all of that stress and financial worry. With no obligations to be anywhere until Sunday morning mass, this was a day for Trojans football, a day for playing with the kids, a day for relaxing with a good book, a day for—

"The lawn desperately needs to be mowed, Louie," Terry called out from the kitchen.

"What'd Mom say, Ray?" Louie asked his oldest son, whom he was trying to teach the USC fight song in the living room.

"Mow the lawn," Ray said.

"Could you hear me, Louie?" Terry called again. "The whole family is coming over tomorrow, remember?"

"Yeah!" Louie said. "I'll get on that."

"Thank you, Poopsie."

Of course, the downside of having shot eardrums was the whole not-being-able-to-hear-much part. Also, his hearing aid was a large cumbersome device worn around the neck—not exactly a desirable fashion statement for twenty-seven-year-olds.

On this day, however, the hearing aid would come in quite handy.

Louie checked his watch: quarter after ten—still a good hour before the pregame show. Still plenty of time to get that lawn mowed. Still plenty of time to teach Ray the last two lines of "Fight On," too. Heck, still enough time in there to scan a little of the *LA Times*'s game coverage—not *all* of the coverage, just the breakdown of the game's key plotlines, and maybe a quick glance at the position-by-position matchups, and maybe a little lookie-lookie at—

"Louie, I'm looking at the lawn out there and it isn't getting any shorter with you in your chair," Terry announced from the kitchen.

"Okay, okay," he replied, folding the newspaper. "I'm working on it right now."

He gave Terry a love pat on his way out to the garage.

"Thank you." She sighed. This was not a day for procrastination. She hated to nag him—this was a rare day off for her busy, hardworking husband—but with five loads of laundry to wash, two bathrooms to clean, and one delicious yet nutritious meal for twelve guests to prepare before the end of the day, a reminder or two seemed reasonable. She cringed, already anticipating her mother-in-law's shrill voice: "Terry, why does your yard look like a rain forest?" "Terry, when is the last time you combed your hair?" "Terry, when is the last time you dusted your spice rack?" No, reminders are justified today, she thought.

"Oh boy," Louie muttered, spying his old rusted push mower beneath a pile of garage junk, spiderwebs spanning between its handles. "What happened to my day off?" He thought of the neighbor's brand-new motorized lawn mower, how nice it would be to afford one of those beauties someday. "Shoot, if I had one like the Jacksons', I'd mow the lawn every single day," he mused, grabbing a metal file from the tool bench. As he sat down to file the mower's blades, he heard Terry call him.

"Louie, when you get done sharpening your axe, can you grab me your work shirts? I'm doing laundry."

"I'll get them for you now," he said, happy for the excuse to get out of the cold garage.

Louie did intend to return to his mower work, but then he saw the time, eleven, and figured a little listen to the pregame radio show wouldn't hurt as long as he didn't get sucked in. As long as they weren't saying anything interesting about USC's strategy. As long as they didn't interview Coach Clark about the Trojans' week of practice and preparation. As long as his favorite recliner didn't seem so dang comfortable. As long as his wife didn't noti—

"Louie!" Terry shouted from behind an armload of laundered diapers. When his name started with an alto and ended in a falsetto, Louie knew he was in for a spirited conversation. "You have been putting this off all day. You cannot watch the game until the lawn is mowed—"

"But I wasn't watching it." Louie tried to squeeze in an excuse. "I was just listening to some—"

"Then you're going to finish listening and that'll turn into watching and before we know it my parents are here and your mother is here and she's complaining . . ."

"I said I'll get on it," he tried again. "I do work two jobs, you know."

"You say you're on it, but you're never on it. You always put it off and then it never happens. . . ."

Louie had heard enough. The carping words were rattling off

so fast they blended together. "I'm not going to put up with this baloney," he thought. "The only thing I *always* do is work my butt off and if she's not going to listen to me . . ." With a stealthy yet casual-looking reach to his hearing aid, he turned Terry's volume down . . .

". . . and I can just hear the Jacksons now, asking the Schmidts if they've ever seen a more horrible lawn, thinking maybe they oughta show mercy on us and come mow the lawn for us . . ."

"Ahh, *silence*," Louie thought, proud of his cunning, "but why'd she stop talking? And what's that violent look in her eye? I haven't seen that one be— *Uh-oh*."

The volume adjustment hadn't been stealthy enough. Terry had seen it and his ensuing lack of response. She'd figured out that he'd put her on mute. And she was not thrilled.

There were thirteen doors in the house and within sixty seconds Terry had slammed every one.

Louie didn't need his hearing aid to sense the house shaking, and when the tornado of Terry's fury hit the kitchen, banging cupboards and drawers and doors along the way, Louie decided he'd be safer if he left the house for a while.

Walking across his front lawn, the first thing he noticed was that the grass really needed to be mowed, especially next to the Jacksons' wonder lawn. Then he noticed how far the cracking sound of slammed cupboards could carry down the street. With his hands in his pockets, he shuffled his feet down the sidewalk, kicking pebbles, until another realization hit him: "That was plain dumb, Louie," he told himself. Louie's pride replied, *Yeah, well, she knows better than to nag you—you said you'd do it! How many days off have you had this year? Who's paying the bills? Who barely gets to see the kids? Besides all that, who's fighting the Irish today?*

"Now that's even dumber, Louie," he told himself. "This is your wife we're talking about, bud. Get your act together and go apologize."

Meanwhile, Terry was taking her anger out on the kitchen floor. Gripping the mop so tightly her knuckles turned white, her ego fumed: *How dare he treat you like that! He knows better than that. You work your behind off all day, all week, just to get this house decent looking. You deserve respect!* With plenty of kindling left to burn, she moved to the kitchen walls and began to scrub them so feverishly that the paint nearly came off.

As the anger slowly subsided, she began to analyze the fight with Louie from every angle, all two of them, which was already double the angles she'd been able to see while whacking the floor with the mop. She thought about how important that silly game had been to him, how he'd been talking about it all week, and how fortunate he'd felt finally to have a day off from work. The image of Louie in the living room, trying to steer Ray into Trojan mania, made her smile a little, even if she'd been trying not to. "What he did was totally uncalled for," she thought to herself, "but I could've handled that so much better."

Her ego was about to make a rebuttal when a timid knock sounded from the front door.

"Mind you, I was knocking at my own front door," Louie explains with a big smile, "and I tell her how sorry I—"

"He's standing there with this sheepish look," Terry cuts in, "holding a red rose in his hand, and I couldn't . . ." She cringes. "Shoot! There I go again."

Louie nods forgivingly.

"See, I still cut him off," she continues. "Fifty-five years later and we're still working on being respectful to each other."

"It is easy to forget sometimes," Louie agrees. "But respect in a marriage is giving your spouse the highest esteem you can give. It is the key to open communication by listening with your mind and listening with your heart."

"Also, we never forget to say 'Sorry' to each other—and mean it—whenever we fail to be considerate of each other's feelings." She looks to Louie. "Sorry, honey."

Louie accepts the apology with his big, gentle smile. "The only thing I try to forget," he says with a chuckle, "is how bad those Trojans got whooped up on that day."

Chapter 7

What's the Secret to Staying in Love for a Lifetime?

FOUR-LETTER WORD

—by Jason

"Fellas, this is all you need to know to make a love last," said Reverend Thomas, our first Marriage Master interviewee.

I leaned in, eager to hear his secret.

"Love is a four-letter word spelled G-I-V-E."

And? Could you perhaps G-I-V-E me something more useful than that, Reverend? I'd expect something a little more profound from a man of the cloth.

The search for secrets to lifelong marriage really comes down to one question for me: *How do I make love last?* After all, how many marriages end with this statement: "I just didn't feel the same way about her anymore"? How many of *my* relationships have ended with that statement?

This is the concern almighty for short-run lovers like me: Where *does* love go?

I close my eyes and remember the first time I fell in love. I was in college. We were driving along Oregon's country roads in the springtime, surrounded by fields painted green and luminescent yellow. The sun hovered near the horizon. I rolled down the windows of my Honda Civic and popped open the sunroof. The Pixies' "Where Is My Mind?" wailed from the speakers. My girlfriend's curly hair was blowing around, out of control. My hand was sandwiched between her hand and her thigh. I looked at her. She looked at me. She smiled and put her head on my shoulder. A rush of emotion made my heart pound with joy. "This is it," I told myself. "This is love. I'm in love. I want to feel like this forever!" I had visions of curly-haired, laughing children. I saw us going the distance. I scanned the realms of possibility: How could this amazing, gorgeous, brilliant creature have walked the earth all these years without my knowing? How could someone this magnificent possibly want me? And yet, she did!

Two years later, I told her I didn't want to be with her anymore. Yeah, she was still pretty and bright and all that amazing stuff, but no more so than other women who had the added advantage of being mysteriously unfamiliar to me. Life together had grown routine. Her mere presence no longer transported me to euphoria. I couldn't even summon giddy if I wanted to. "I'm sorry," I told her, "I just don't feel like I'm in love with you anymore."

Based on my own experiences and those of my friends, single, married, and single again, I had begun wondering if lifelong love might just be a fairy tale. Naturally, the thing I couldn't wait to hear from these dynamic duos married forty, fifty, even sixty years was their secret to staying madly in love. Surely they would offer more of a blueprint than Reverend Thomas, who, when pressed to elaborate, just shook his head and smiled at me.

Imagine my disappointment when couple after couple just sat there, sweet, thoughtful, patient with us, often offering cookies. But sizzling? Giddy? All over each other? Hardly. At first, I wasn't sure if the interviewees understood what love was *really.*

"You think they're still in love?" I'd ask Mat after every interview.

"Is that a rhetorical question?" he'd reply. "Of course they're in love."

"They barely looked at each other, maybe ten times. Even then it was more a glance. I don't think they are."

"You don't know. They may have arthritic necks."

"Must have arthritic lips then, too, because they kiss like woodpeckers."

"Did you see how he smoothed out the pillow cushions for her? They held hands the whole time. And didn't you notice the way she laughed when he told the knock-knock joke that wasn't funny? They're still together and they're still happy. That's love."

"That's not love. Force of habit, maybe, marriage, maybe— but not love."

Surely that's not love, I told myself. And surely I was the best judge of such matters, the stud of love with all of those multiple months of serious relationship experience to rely upon for his wise, judicious claims. "Nope, I know love and that's *not* it."

To me, then, love was like a Halloween costume: The red, one-piece bear-cat suit hides in my closet all year, but for one night, I am transformed into someone completely different, who is wild and crazy and giddy . . . and then I forget the costume is there for the next 364 days.

At some point, after interviewing hundreds of couples who refused to conform to my definition of love, it dawned on me that perhaps my model of love might have its drawbacks. I tried to imagine forty-plus years of a dangerous, damaging, slightly out-of-reach relationship that required me to don a red bear-cat costume and ultimately left me in the dark and it sounded . . . not good.

"Sounds like you think love is purely a feeling," more than one Marriage Master told me. *Well, yes* . . . The problem with my definition, they pointed out, is that feelings change. Deadlines, traffic, the weather, the number of bills stacked up on the kitchen table can alter how we feel about anything on any given day. Time changes feelings, too. Growing up, I hated broccoli. Now I want broccoli trees in my backyard I love it so much. The problem with defining love as a feeling, the Marriage Masters told me, is that you get blindsided by the incredible passion that rules the early stage of a relationship. That's the stage when everything your partner says is brilliant and witty and the very sound of her voice makes you understand the appeal of old musicals, when the besotted hero runs down the street and breaks into song. You want to feel that way forever. But marriage doesn't run on adrenaline.

The Marriage Masters told me that this heady infatuation stage doesn't last, but its ending signals a critical juncture. Either giddy passion becomes so conspicuous by its absence it's clear that's all there was, or you realize your heart is no less full when the palpitations cease.

David and Sheila Epstein, married fifty years, literally wrote the book on marriage. Halfway through our interview, they pulled out their book, *The Art of Engagement,* and showed me the stages of love, the first two of which I knew well: illusion (my favorite), and then disillusionment, when I started noticing my mate's flaws, fretted about her dwindling adoration of me, and became more of a "me-some" than a "we-some."

Much to my surprise, the Epsteins indicated that virtually all loving couples go through these stages. But the third takes more effort: decision. That's when you realize love is not just a feeling. Love is a choice, a decision to act loving, no matter what. Love is a decision to give to your partner, putting her needs first.

For someone who's infatuated with infatuation, like me, the third stage was of epic proportions. The breakdown of the three stages helped me understand that my relationships aren't necessarily doomed because I'm no longer walking on air.

Greg and Marlyn Lincoln have been married more than forty-two years. I admire Greg, especially because he had the courage to admit he had at one time fallen out of love with his wife, or at least that's how he perceived it at the time. The two were married about twenty years, when Greg realized he was bored. His heart no longer raced at the sight of her. She never put the cap back on the toothpaste, which annoyed him to no end. In a rush to leave for work in the morning, he sometimes forgot to kiss her good-bye, after vowing on his honeymoon he would rather die than start the day without their morning kiss. Worse yet, he didn't particularly miss the kiss. He looked at the woman he'd vowed to cherish forever and panicked: "What's wrong with me? Am I with the wrong person? Why don't I love her anymore?"

I related 100 percent. I wanted to jump out of my chair and give the guy a big hug to celebrate our newfound kinship: *That's the same kind of crap love's been pulling on me!* But, unlike me, Greg made the decision to stay put in his commitment; he waited for the tide to return. "Two months later," he said, "I awakened with a sudden rush of feelings, as if my love was a beautiful flower blossoming again. And I'm so glad that I didn't throw in the towel just because my feelings had disappeared for a bit because I can't imagine not being with her now—I cherish her. She means everything to me." Greg was the first of many interviewees who pointed out the ebb-and-flow nature of love in married life. I'm not exactly thrilled to learn about the outgoing tide of feeling part, but I did take heart that an ebb is not an end; the love will find a flow again. The secret they taught me is to *be* loving even when I don't feel loving. Emotions follow behavior.

What's your secret to staying in love all these years? We asked that question again and again. One of my favorite answers came from Mim and Sherman Andelson, married fifty-seven years. "First of all," Mim replied, "you have to define what love is."

I was tempted to tell her about my Halloween costume metaphor but opted instead to shut up and listen for once.

Sherman looked at his wife, maybe to see if he should go first, then to Mat and me. "Let me tell you what love means to me. If I see something beautiful, and I see it by myself, my first thought is, 'I wish Mim were here.' Nothing is beautiful alone. It's beautiful only when you look at it with somebody else. And if that someone else is Mim, then it's *really* beautiful. A beautiful picture, a beautiful beach, a quiet interlude where you're sipping coffee—I will never forget those afternoons I'd meet Mim for coffee in the student union at the University of—"

"I do, too!" Mim interrupted. "Except I remember you always brought the newspaper and read the sports section while I was there, which I didn't like."

The way Sherman reacted to the interruption and criticism

was something to remember: He smiled. Looking again at his wife, he continued, "Love doesn't go away. It may become obscured by problems and arguments and issues to work out, but once you work them out you find that you're just as much in love. So this fear that 'I'm going to fall out of love' is a false fear. I know I've never fallen out of love; it only gets better and better and better. It doesn't fade. It just gets better."

Talking to the Andelsons was probably the closest experience I'd had to Mat's "that's the marriage I want" moment with his grandparents. The Andelsons aren't just a lifelong couple—they are lifelong lovers. I realize that lifelong love is less the giddy, passionate kiss and more Sherman's gentle, patient smile. It is finding and sharing the moments made beautiful only because of the special person who's been at your side forever.

That's how I'll G-I-V-E my wife.

Heads or Tails

Jerry and Patti Hempenius
Married 51 years

Patti Hempenius knew well the pros and cons of HMOs, PPOs, and POS plans. She knew the name, location, and function of all four lobes of the human brain. She knew how to operate cannulae, speculums, and state-of-the-art EKG machines. She knew how to calm a four-year-old child enough to take a blood sample. She even knew how to read three different doctors' handwriting. But how to pull weeds without leaving the roots behind? Now, that was the $64,000 question.

"Why . . . won't . . . you . . . come . . . *ahh!*"   she   shrieked, catching herself from falling backward, bits of mangled stalk clenched in her fist. "Out."

This was January 1976, a new year and a new set of challenges for Patti, these darn rebellious weeds, for one. She scanned a green trail of shredded foliage along the outskirts of the Villager Motel parking lot, eyeing her failed attempts to free the strangled flower bed. She wiped the sweat from her eyes with the sleeve of her baggy, teal Morro Bay sweatshirt and attacked another weed. This time, she dug around it, holding the stalk at its base, and slowly eased it out clean, roots and all.

She thought about her old staff at the hospital when she'd told them about the life change she and her husband would be making. The doctors, shaking their heads half amused, half disappointed: "Nurses are supposed to work in the *hospital* industry, not the *hospitality* industry." The nurses and patients, all asking the same question, "Are you sure you're really making the right decision?" in six hundred different ways. Remembering their expressions gave her a new resolve.

"I can do this," she said.

Patti never had been one to back down from a challenge. She'd decided early on that she was going to be the best nurse in the world. By the time she finished high school, several top nursing colleges had accepted her to do just that. Her tenacity had enabled her to achieve most everything she wanted in life.

If there was such a thing as a male equivalent to her strong-willed personality, she'd found him during a visit to check out Southern California universities.

After a long week of campus tours, Patti and a girlfriend eagerly accepted an invitation to a lakeside Campus Crusade barbecue. Summer was on its way. College kids frolicked on the grass, laughing and flirting, taking advantage of the sun's warm rays. Patti and her friend were in the middle of it all, moving from picnic blanket to picnic blanket to meet new people. And every time Patti turned around there was this smiling kid named Jerry.

Sitting next to Patti on a small motorboat late that afternoon, Jerry slyly tried to sneak his arm around her shoulders. She immediately responded with a splash of lake water to the face. She had a boyfriend, after all, and even if he did live hundreds of miles away, a handful of icy water in this smiling kid's mug sent just the message she intended: *I'm not easy, buster.*

Jerry went home that night and told his mother he'd found his wife. "I don't know how yet, Ma, but by golly I'm going to marry this girl."

Jerry stood before a large church audience, prepared to sing the Lord's Prayer hymn. His angelic tenor had paid for his college, so by now he was a fairly seasoned pro at performing in front of big groups like this one. But for the first time in his life—despite the fact that he'd probably said this prayer ten thousand times since childhood—his mind completely blanked on the words. His bride, Patti, took his hand and smiled gently. "Our Father, who art in heaven," she whispered. Jerry sang the line, majestically, and looked to her for more help. "Hallowed be thy name," she whispered again. Back and forth, line by line, they finished the prayer together. Not one eye was dry in the pews when the minister started his pronouncement: "I could not imagine a more beautiful way to start a marriage."

Together, they were a powerful team.

And now, here she was in the parking lot of a motel. Some days, even an old sweatshirt felt too fancy for some of the duties she had to perform. She shuddered, thinking of Room 211. She'd knocked on the door and announced herself, "Housekeeping!" No answer. She opened the door . . . and froze. Half-eaten cheeseburgers and fries scattered across the floor. Alarm clock radio blaring David Bowie's "Space Oddity" full blast. Bedsheets in a ball in the half-full bathtub—for what reason, Patti did not want to know, nor did she want to clean it.

"Why am I here?" she asked herself.

Patti had been a superbly respected head nurse in charge of a private practice cardiac department. Six full-time staff, seventy-five hundred patients, and three highly paid, highly educated brains behind stethoscopes were all in her orchestrated care. She loved the people around her. It was her dream come true, especially in contrast to this Room 211 nightmare. Now, she was a guest-checking, noise complaint–remedying, television-fixing, laundry-washing, weed-pulling, disinfectant-spraying, motel owner/operator. She'd agreed to this challenge—the payoff had seemed worth her sacrifice—but, still, she couldn't help feeling a bit resentful. "Here I am, on my hands and knees, scrubbing toilets," she thought, "while Jerry's up there in his cushy chair at his cushy desk in his ivory palace."

She wondered if Jerry could possibly comprehend the full extent of her sacrifice, of this gift she was giving him. With a deep breath, she slid a surgical mask over her mouth and nose, and donned her rubber gloves. "I *love* my husband, I *love* my husband, I love my *husband,*" she muttered as if it were a mantra.

Jerry's ambition had always rivaled Patti's. By the age of seven, he had already built a very successful chicken-brooding business. He bought baby chicks, then fed and raised them, slaughtered them, plucked them, and sold them to the market for a profit. At eight years old, he started a produce business on the side and soon became the best vegetable salesman the neighborhood had ever seen. With his earnings he bought clothes, games, a bike, even his own dog. The more his start-ups thrived, the more he thrived; his entrepreneurial spirit defined him.

Later, he got a master's degree in retailing and rapidly rose from sales clerk to general manager at a major department store. The ongoing promotions up the ladder made him feel good and the money afforded his family a great life, but when corporate offered him the next rung up, to regional sales manager, he realized he'd hit a ceiling, if only a self-imposed one. His time with Patti and the kids was already too limited for his taste; the position's nonstop travel would steal more. On top of this, the idea that he'd used his intelligence, creativity, prowess, and decades of energy to build someone else's business dream burned his gut. After twenty years in the rat race, Jerry's entrepreneurial spirit was screaming to be resurrected. But what could he do? God knows chicken brooding wouldn't put the kids through college.

Then one night, Jerry burst through the kitchen door. "I think I've got it, Patti!" he called out. The enthusiasm in his voice caught her off guard. And his smile was so full of his famously infectious spirit! Patti hadn't seen him smile like that for, well, way too long.

"How about owning a hotel together!" he continued.

Patti didn't know what to say. "Um, I don't know, Jerry."

He rattled off the inspiration details a million miles an hour. CPA friend. Smartest guy I know. Bought a hotel. Best business move he's ever made. You and me. So happy.

She shuffled her feet, too fond of that smile to shoot him down. She thought of his unhappiness. While she typically hurried the kids off to school so she could get to the doctors' office sooner, he trudged around in the mornings, dreading another day at the store. Patti would come home feeling more energized than when she'd left; Jerry, just more desperate for a change. Patti had been searching for something she could do to help him, something to get his ambitious spirit back, but this definitely wasn't the "something" she'd had in mind.

"It sounds . . . I don't know," she said.

Jerry gave her a huge hug, thankful at least for her willing consideration.

A few months later, they visited a small, picturesque fishing village on the central California coast to help Patti's parents move. The family-owned cafés looked out at the pristine shores and the friendly locals were quick to stop and chat. Charmed by the peaceful ambience, Jerry and Patti fell in love with Morro Bay. On a whim, Jerry hired a broker to look for businesses in the area. When a small, two-story, twenty-two-unit motel came up,

Jerry and Patti put in a lowball offer, thinking it would never get accepted.

Within twenty-four hours, the offer was approved: $385,000, the Villager Motel is yours.

"Oh yes!" Jerry said, exploding with excitement.

"Oh no!" Patti thought, stunned.

She'd known that going along with this venture—if only in an appeasing sort of way—would *eventually* force her to make changes. But this was *now*! Too many risks! Too many questions! Three *hundred* and eighty-five *thousand*? Where are we going to come up with that? Sell the house? But I love my home! What about the custom Grecian pool with Jacuzzi waterfall? We just put it in! Do we have to live at the motel? We don't know anything about motels! What if it fails? And the biggest, scariest question: What about my career? I *love* my career.

Jerry eased her mind about the money. He made a strong case for how successful they could be in the motel industry. She had no problems trusting his business capabilities. But when Jerry suggested that she quit her job right away so she could move up to Morro Bay and take over the operation solo, she had some issues.

"Why am *I* the one who has to move up there first?" she asked. "This is *your* idea!"

"I know, but if I move up there right now, then we won't get my January bonus," he beseeched.

He had a point. The bonus was a major chunk of change. "But I don't know the first thing about running a motel," she said. "You're the entrepreneur."

"Yes, and I'll help with all the business stuff over the phone," he rebutted. "But you've run a private practice for twenty years—cleanliness and service are your strongest suits."

Dammit, he had a point again. "But what about my department? My doctors? My staff? I can't just leave them high and dry like that. They'll need two people to do my job, maybe more! They'll self-destruct! They'll think I'm crazy!" she said. "Plus, I'll miss them."

Sitting across the kitchen table in their spacious home, Patti and Jerry Hempenius stared at each other with the frustrated, frazzled looks of presidential candidates near the end of a four-hour televised debate. Neither could find an easy solution; neither could find anything new to say. It was a stalemate between a husband and a wife who cared deeply for each other but had never been the type to compromise their individual ambitions.

Jerry reached into his pocket and found a quarter. He looked to Patti for her approval. She stared at him in a daze, the implications flying around inside her mind like a swarm of screeching bats. She tried to boil it down, to make sense of it all. Finally, she thought, "My husband is more important to me than my career. I want him to be happy. I *love* my husband."

She nodded her head to Jerry. "Heads."

Jerry flipped the coin. Tails.

Patti squeezed out the best smile she could muster and gave her husband a hug, then called her doctors that night: "I'm moving to Morro Bay to run a motel." They thought she was kidding at first, crazy second. She couldn't fully disagree, but she made the decision not to act bitter, no matter how difficult that was. After all, Patti had never backed down from a challenge, she reminded herself as she knelt beside the flower bed.

Months later, Patti was admiring her stack of freshly folded sheets in the Villager Motel's laundry room when Jerry pulled into the parking lot, honking his horn and waving and grinning. It was June now and he'd been coming up to help her every other weekend throughout the spring, but the house had just sold. He was ready to launch full-time into his dream venture and couldn't be any happier. Like a Little Leaguer cheering his teammate's game-winning home run, he shouted as he ran to meet her with a big bear hug, "The place looks great!"

He held his arm around her shoulders while she walked him on a tour of the motel improvements she'd made over the three months. Not one weed touched her flower beds. The maids never showed up drunk anymore. Occupancy rates were on the rise. Guest complaints were almost zero. Business cards from inquiring investors stacked tall.

She told him about the twenty Hell's Angels who'd shown up at her desk late one night. "I told them, 'Look, gentlemen, I have rules here: There will be *no* drinking, *no* parties, *no* smoking indoors, *no* fighting, *no* horseplay, and absolutely *no* bikes in the rooms!'"

"Oh, no." He winced. "What'd they do?"

"They acted like gentlemen," she replied, "and thanked me for the 'most pleasant stay' on their way out."

Jerry shot her a proud, passion-filled look. The old fire was in his eyes. Patti beamed, also proud of the success she'd built, but even prouder of the sacrifice she'd made for her husband, the man she most definitely loved. He could have thanked her a hundred times for what she'd given him—and he would—but that never felt half as rewarding as it did to have her smiling kid named Jerry back.

The Hempeniuses, now married fifty-one years, have owned and eventually sold nine successful motels. They spend most of their time vacationing but often have to come out of retirement to take on new challenges. On this day, lounging peacefully on the balcony of their beachfront timeshare villa, Patti tries to convince Jerry to go to the beach instead of his preference, the pool. Jerry is happy to defer to her. "Marriage is all about give and take," he says.

"Absolutely," Patti agrees. "There have been times when it felt like I was giving ninety percent and taking only ten, but Jerry has done the same for me. That's what love is: selflessness for the sake of our marriage."

"Over the course of a lifetime together, it all evens out. We're one heck of a team. We have been since day one."

"It's been a beautiful adventure," Patti says, reaching for Jerry's hand. "I wouldn't change a thing."

"Love You"

Dirk and Ruthie Dirksen
Married 58 years

The first note was hidden in the back of Dirk's dresser drawer, between the heavy dark gray sweater Dirk wore only when the temperature dropped below freezing and the itchy blue wool one he refused to wear but also refused to throw out, no matter how often Ruthie complained about his being a pack rat.

It was a chilly morning, and even though it was barely October, the forecast on the news station Dirk listened to while he got ready for work predicted the first snowfall of the season. He pulled the gray sweater over his head, and a tiny folded piece of paper that had been tucked into one of the sleeves fell to the floor.

"Must be an old receipt," he figured, bending down and picking it up. He was about to toss it into the trash can when he hesitated. "A receipt wouldn't be folded so precisely, would it?" His puzzlement turned into a wide grin as he unfolded the scrap and saw what was written on it.

"I love you."

Three words, neatly printed in Ruthie's careful, tight handwriting.

He could hear Ruthie in the kitchen, humming along with

the radio as she fixed their breakfast, and his smile grew even bigger.

"When the heck did she write this?" he wondered, smoothing the creases out of the note. He hadn't opened that drawer since the previous spring, when the weather had warmed up and he'd retired the sweater for the summer. She could have hidden the note months ago.

Of course he knew that she loved him—they said "I love you" to each other every day. But seeing it written down, and imagining the happy anticipation Ruthie must have felt when she slipped the note into the back of his sweater drawer, knowing that he'd be surprised to discover it, gave Dirk a joyous rush. It was more than sweet—it was downright romantic.

Not bad for a couple who had already been married more than forty years.

Dirk's first impulse was to rush into the kitchen and sweep Ruthie off her feet, but he stopped himself. There would be plenty of time for kissing later. He had something to do first.

He reached for the pad of paper sitting on the nightstand next to the bed and picked up a pen.

"Thinking of you right now," he wrote on the top sheet, then tore it off and folded it neatly into quarters.

Now all he needed to do was figure out a good place to hide it.

Dirk and Ruthie met in 1946. Ruthie had first noticed the charismatic young man a week earlier, when she was out shopping with a girlfriend and they bumped into a group of boys Ruthie's friend knew.

While her friend chatted with one of the boys, Ruthie stood

off to the side, trying hard not to stare at Dirk. He was horsing around with his buddies, cracking jokes and roughhousing.

Ruthie thought Dirk was completely funny and charming, not to mention as handsome as could be, but before she could work up the nerve to talk to him, Ruthie's friend finished her conversation and the boys moved off. She was disappointed that she hadn't gotten to meet him, but her friend told her not to worry, she'd introduce them the next time they ran into each other.

Happily, Ruthie had to wait only a couple of days. That Saturday night she and her friend went bowling, and who should happen to be in the next lane over but Dirk and his friends!

Ruthie was so nervous about meeting the boy she'd been dreaming of all week that she rolled a gutter ball, but she managed to score something even better. Dirk drove Ruthie home from the bowling alley that night and asked her for a date the next evening.

Ruthie said yes when Dirk asked her to go out with him. And two years later, she said yes again, this time when he asked her to marry him.

Ruthie cut the butter into the flour and began to pinch the pie crust together. Her mind was distracted, but her hands moved with quick, sure precision. After all, she'd been baking Thanksgiving pumpkin pies for the entire fifty years she and Dirk had been married. She didn't even need to consult the recipe, yellowed and tattered on a pumpkin-stained index card.

She could make this pie in her sleep, she thought, adding a tablespoon of cold water to the dough and mixing it in. Although if she *was* sleeping, she wished she'd wake up and find out that the doctor's verdict was nothing but a bad dream.

Dirk had been diagnosed with pulmonary fibrosis. And as much as Ruthie wanted to believe she was dreaming, she knew that she was wide awake, and the nightmare was real.

Ever since Dirk had gotten sick, he'd grown more dependent on Ruthie to take care of him. She did so naturally, unhesitatingly, and was happy to do it. But it was hard to see her once-vibrant husband too weak to change out of his robe, and the holidays, which were supposed to be such a time of joy, were especially difficult.

Ruthie dusted some flour onto the counter and began to roll out her pie crust.

One of Dirk and Ruthie's favorite activities to do together was going for a drive. Ever since the night they met, when Dirk drove Ruthie home from the bowling alley in his old Chevy coupe, the couple would pile into the front seat of the car and cruise through the small pretty towns nearby, past the fields and meadows of the countryside where they lived, traveling wherever the road and their sense of adventure took them.

Ruthie had never learned how to drive, so Dirk had the wheel and she was in charge of the radio. She would snuggle up next to him, their fingers intertwined, her head resting on his shoulder, as the scenery flew past.

They went for drives most evenings, after Dirk got home from work, but they especially loved going for rides at Christmastime, when the night was lit up by the festive colored lights decorating houses and buildings.

"Guess we won't be seeing the lights this year," Ruthie thought, reaching up to the high cabinet where she kept her collection of pie tins. "It probably won't feel like Christmas without them."

Standing on tiptoe, she grabbed the pie tin she wanted, bracing her other hand against the ones piled on top of it to keep them from falling. She tugged the tin free, and a piece of paper that had been tucked inside it fluttered down onto the counter.

She picked up the speck of paper and carefully brushed the flour off of it before unfolding it.

"You're beautiful," read the note, in Dirk's characteristic messy scrawl.

Ruthie leaned against the counter, her worries forgotten for one blissful moment. Ever since she had written Dirk that first note ten years earlier, the couple had been trading them back and forth, writing out short-but-sweet messages and hiding them in unexpected places.

"Love you."

"Dreaming of you."

"XOXO."

Sometimes it would take a month or two for the other person to find the note, but he or she always wrote one back, picking a new hiding place.

It was a simple pleasure, but it delighted both of them just the same. In the half century they had been married, they had weathered some rough times, Dirk's illness being the latest and toughest of them all, but in fifty years, they had never stopped loving each other. The notes were a small but tangible reminder of this, breaking up the day-to-day routine of married life with conscious declarations of their feelings.

The notes helped fuel their love, and on this difficult Thanksgiving at least, gave Ruthie strength. No matter what trials they'd have to face with Dirk's diagnosis, they'd get through them together.

Ruthie wiped her hands on the blue-striped dish towel and wrote a note for Dirk. She picked a hiding place, and once the note was safely sequestered, returned to her baking, humming a Christmas carol as she settled the pie crust into its tin.

"Oh!" Dirk's eyes lit up as Ruthie walked into the bedroom. "There's my angel!"

Ruthie smiled, managing to hide the tears that lately were always threatening to erupt.

Dirk's health had been declining steadily since the holidays. He underwent a triple bypass operation, but still continued to get sicker. He no longer left the house; most days he was unable even to leave his bed.

Ruthie lay down on the bed next to him, curving her body around his, wrapping her arms around his thin body and spooning him. For as long as they had been married, Ruthie and Dirk slept in this position, cuddling as they fell asleep.

Neither of them had ever understood couples who went to bed at different times. Why would anyone choose to stay up and watch TV when he or she could be spooning? Even after Dirk got sick, Ruthie still went to bed when he did, regardless of what the clock said or how wide awake she felt. She didn't want to miss the chance to be together, to hold him close.

"My angel," Dirk repeated. He sighed contentedly, snuggling back against her. "Through all our years together, we always managed to stay in love with each other," he told her.

The tears threatened to spill over, but Ruthie squeezed her eyes tightly, forcing them back.

"You're the only one I ever loved," she answered, tightening her arms around her husband. "My only love."

Three days later, on March 10, 2003, Dirk passed away.

He was lying in bed with Ruthie behind him, spooning him, stroking his face, trying to remember every moment, every feeling, every detail of the man she'd loved for more than fifty years.

As they lay together, Dirk's breathing slowed, growing fainter, until eventually, quietly, gently, it stopped.

Now the tears came. Ruthie stayed with Dirk for another fifteen minutes, crying, cuddling him, and telling him how much she loved him.

Ruthie didn't know how she was going to live without him. Days turned into weeks, and then into months, and still Ruthie felt alone, desolate, unable to fathom how she was going to live her life alone.

Then one morning in June, Ruthie was in her bedroom, listlessly cleaning out the drawer where she kept her summer clothes, a chore she usually undertook in the springtime but hadn't been able to summon the energy to do this year.

As she reached into the back of the drawer for a crumpled linen sundress, her fingers touched a piece of paper. Ruthie's hand shook as she pulled it out and looked at it.

On the paper, written in shaky letters, were two words: "Love you."

Dirk had managed to hide one last note for Ruthie before he died. And as she looked at it, Ruthie felt tears come to her eyes. But for the first time in a long time, they weren't tears of pain, but of joy. Joy at the life she had had with Dirk, joy at the love they had shared.

"Love you."

It was the ultimate love note, and like the ones before it, it gave Ruthie strength. As much as she missed Dirk, Ruthie realized that she wasn't alone. She still had his love.

She was holding proof of it.

Ruthie has since framed the final love note under her favorite photo, one of Dirk smiling, holding her in his arms on the couch. She looks at the final "love you" note every day as a reminder of their everlasting love story. "Staying in love for a lifetime is natural," she says. "The love was just in me and it was in him, too.

" 'Until death do us part' just doesn't seem to apply to us."

Our Final Road Trip

Derrick and Merideth Townsend
Married 65 years

Mile 1: Worcester, MA

Derrick Townsend wheeled Merideth's chair to the passenger side of their old Buick, then squatted down, his knees creakily protesting, so his face was level with hers.

"You want to sit in the front seat so you can watch the scenery, or the backseat so you can stretch out?" he asked his wife.

Merideth looked back at him blankly, wobbling her head slightly at the sting of the brisk spring air against her pale cheek.

Derrick waited a second, not really expecting an answer, then smiled. "Scenery it is!" he proclaimed, his back joining his knees in complaining as he straightened up again. "You can always move to the back if you get tired."

He carefully lifted his wife into the passenger seat, tucking blankets around her to make sure she was warm and as comfortable as possible. He brushed the back of his hand across Merideth's face in a loving caress, marveling at how the soft skin felt just the same as it had the first time he'd touched it, over sixty-five years before.

Merideth was about to celebrate her 102nd birthday, and

Derrick, ninety-four, was determined that she do it in the place in the world she loved best: Medford, Oregon, more than 3,100 miles away.

Early in their marriage, Derrick and Merideth had taken a road trip up and down the West Coast. Out of all the places they drove through and visited, from Southern California to Canada, Merideth had fallen head over heels in love with Medford, Oregon. They'd spent only one night there, but ever since then she had always recalled fond memories of Medford's trees, its rivers, its countryside.

Derrick eased himself into the driver's seat. He glanced at the stack of road maps and took a deep breath. It was going to be a long drive to Oregon, but he couldn't wait to get started. So he gave Merideth a smile, turned the key in the ignition, and just like that, they were on their way.

Mile 250: Allentown, PA

Derrick yawned, flicking on his turn signal and moving into the right lane of the highway. Merideth was napping in the seat next to him, and he knew that if he didn't want to fall asleep too, he needed to get some coffee. As tough as it was getting Merideth situated in and out of her wheelchair, he knew that would be nothing to the trouble he'd face if he dozed off behind the wheel. So when he spotted a sign for a rest area, he pulled the car over and got out, savoring the stretch of his legs after sitting for so long, then moved around to the trunk to fetch Merideth's wheelchair.

Once they were seated in a cozy booth in the diner, his drowsiness was quickly replaced by the pleasure of a fresh, hot cup of java and still-warm slice of cherry pie. While Merideth devoured her pie in slow, steady bites, Derrick leaned back, relaxing against the padded vinyl banquette, remembering the first time he'd sat across from Merideth in a diner.

It was 1942. Merideth had been recruited by her church to write letters to the U.S. servicemen fighting in World War II. At random, she selected a Navy submarine sailor named Derrick Townsend as her penpal. Their correspondence, anonymous in the beginning, soon became very personal, despite the fact that Derrick, who didn't have much faith in his own penmanship, was relying on his submarine mate to do the writing. When the war ended they agreed to meet in a New York diner to see if there would be any chemistry in person. There was plenty indeed—enough to last them for a lifetime.

Mile 1,000: Joliet, IL

Before the sun even peeked over the horizon, Derrick pulled the car up to the motel room door. Even though it was very early in the morning, he couldn't wait to get back on the road. Besides, he hadn't been able to sleep much the night before. Merideth's pain had grown steadily worse through the night, each groaning breath more effective than any alarm clock. Derrick loaded their suitcases in the trunk, then crossed to the bed where Merideth was lying, glassy-eyed with pain, a slight sheen of sweat coating her skin.

"Come on, sweetheart," he whispered, smoothing her hair back from her forehead and then lifting her into his arms.

His own pain—the aches in his joints, the stiffness in his back, the throbbing behind his eyes from too much time focused on the road—was forgotten as his wife let out a little mewl of discomfort.

"I could put the man in jail," he thought, picturing the doctor in Worcester who had been seeing Merideth for a long-standing bladder ailment. "Three years we visited him and he did nothing for her." His jaw set in a grim line as he thought about the ordeal they had gone through. Worcester itself had become the embodiment of their numerous frustrations with the city's retirement homes, social workers, and medical care facilities. He was happy to put it behind him, eager to put as much distance as he could between themselves and the place that had caused them so much agony.

"Shhh," he soothed, as Merideth let out another cry. "We're almost there. We'll be in Medford before you know it."

Mile 2,250: Logan, UT

Derrick glanced into the rearview mirror, watching the slow, peaceful rise and fall of his wife's chest as she finally found some relief in sleep. Every muscle in his body screamed for him to pull the car over, take a break, ease the white-hot cramps that speared through his legs, his shoulders, his neck from sitting in one position for so long, but he kept his hands on the wheel and his eyes on the road. If he pulled over, it might wake Merideth, and he refused to let that happen. A couple of twinges in his body he could endure. But seeing his wife hurting? Not if there was anything in the world he could do about it.

He had seen all the suffering he could take that day at the hospital in Worcester. Merideth's pain had reached such intensity that Derrick could no longer lift her into the car. Frantic, he dialed 911 and an ambulance took her immediately to the emergency room.

They arrived at twelve but were informed that everybody

was at lunch until one. "She has great pain!" he told them, but lunch seemed to be more important than the patients.

After three hours of waiting, Merideth needed to go to the bathroom. Derrick scurried around the hospital, asking everyone he could find to help his wife get to the bathroom. Everybody gave him the same answer: "I'll get someone to help you, sir." At five o'clock, still unseen by any doctors and now sitting in her own urine, she ashamedly mumbled: "Take me home, please, Derrick."

Derrick's heart was broken by his wife's miserable countenance. "We need a solution," he thought.

As the Buick cruised over the state line, crossing from Utah into Idaho, Merideth stirred in her sleep, sighing and turning onto her right side.

Derrick bit his lip, watching in the rearview mirror until she settled back down into sleep, and her breathing slowed and steadied again. When he was sure she was still resting comfortably, Derrick smiled.

No sense in stopping now, he thought, rolling his head from side to side to relieve some of the tension in his neck. No sense in stopping when we're so close to the solution.

Mile 3,100: Hayesville, OR

"Wake up, sweetheart," Derrick said softly, as he steered the car off Interstate 5, taking exit 27 to Medford.

Merideth had been sleeping all day, but he knew she wouldn't want to miss this—outside the car window, the setting sun touched the rolling green hills of central Oregon in a blaze of gold, a bright cleansing fire that made the line where land met sky snap and glow.

Merideth sat up, disoriented and sleepy, and Derrick reached across and touched her chin, gently turning her head to the glorious view.

Derrick knew that his wife was no longer able to comprehend much of what was happening around her, and he wasn't sure if she understood that the countryside they were driving through was the same place she had fallen in love with over half a century before. But even if she wasn't aware of that, there was no mistaking the open delight on her face at the sight that greeted her outside the window.

The sun sank below the hills in one last glorious burst of light, but as Derrick looked at his wife, drinking in the gorgeous vista, he felt like now that they had finally arrived in Medford, the sun would never stop shining.

Mile 3,153: Medford, OR

"She wasn't getting the care she needed in Worcester," Derrick told the cheerful young woman in the candy-striped jumper who had come into Merideth's room with an armful of fresh flowers for the nursing home's newest residents.

"So, I packed the Buick up with all of our stuff and told my girl we're going on one last road trip together . . . to Medford, Oregon. A doctor here used machines and electronics to test her and found out the same day that she had a bladder infection. After three weeks of medication, she was cured. Just like that."

"That's wonderful," the candy striper said, beaming at the story's happy ending. She arranged the flowers next to the open window, then plumped up the pillows behind Merideth's head.

"Lunch will be served in an hour in the dining room, but can I get you anything in the meantime?" she asked.

Derrick looked lovingly at his wife, who was sitting up in bed, pink cheeked and pain free, laughing at the way the lace curtains fluttered in the fresh Medford breeze, then turned his gaze to the candy striper, meeting her warm smile with one of his own.

"No, thank you," he answered, reaching for Merideth's hand and clasping it in his own. "I already have everything I need."

Merideth passed away within four months of arriving at her personal utopia in Medford, and Derrick has since moved back to Europe to be with his only remaining family. He doesn't think much of his personal effort to get his wife across the country. "It was her dream," he says. "I would've given her anything."

Chapter 8

What Message Would You Give to the Younger Generations?

A HEART-TO-HEART

—by Mat

"Where do you see yourself one year from today?"

My mom propped her elbows on the white-clothed tabletop and looked from my grandmother to me.

"If you could live any life you wanted," she continued, "what would you be doing this time next year?"

"A year from now? Hmm . . ." I dipped a French fry into ketchup as I thought about it. "Probably teaching high school, livin' in Hillsboro. But I'll spend all my free time traveling— Costa Rica, Mexico, maybe even make it to Rio for Carnivale!"

Mom laughed, leaning back so the waitress could refresh her coffee. Then she turned to my grandmother.

"Okay, Mom, it's your turn," she said.

Grandma stared down at her plate, where her lunch sat, untouched. "I don't—I don't know," she said quietly, shaking her head.

"C'mon, Grandma!" I encouraged. "Sky's the limit! If you could do *anything*—"

She looked up, and I was shocked to see her eyes fill with tears.

"I don't want to be here a year from now! I don't even want to think about it!" Her voice was unnaturally loud, even in the noisy restaurant. "I would rather just die!"

I froze, the French fry halfway to my mouth. I couldn't believe my warm, funny, upbeat grandmother would say such a thing. I knew she'd been having a rough time since Grandpa Jack had died the previous summer. But they had had sixty-three good years together. She had a lifetime of memories with him. Wasn't that enough?

My mom reached out and placed her hand on Grandma's arm. "Mom, what's going on?"

"Jack said that he would never leave me. He promised I would never be alone," Grandma said, her voice quavering. "But he lied! I am so mad at him! How could he break his promise?"

She stared down at her hands, at the wide gold wedding band and sparkling diamond engagement ring, and softly added, "Why didn't he take me with him?"

I felt a lump grow in my throat. I wanted to tell her not to give up, that we wanted her, needed her with us. But I couldn't speak. Neither could my mom.

"The other day I had on a pair of earrings," Grandma said. "But when I reached up to touch the one on my right ear, it was gone. And I started crying, because half of *me* is gone." The tears threatened to overflow as she looked from my mother to me. "I feel like half of me has died. And no one seems to understand. They think I shouldn't be sad, because we had a good long life together. Why would anyone think such a thing? That we had all those years together doesn't make losing him easier. We built our lives around each other!"

I stared down at my plate, guiltily. That was exactly what I had been thinking.

"Jack used to say he'd love me through all eternity; after that I'd be on my own," Grandma continued, with a sad smile. "So now I'm on my own, but by Jack's reckoning, way ahead of schedule."

Watching my grandmother dab at her eyes with her napkin as she tried to compose herself, I realized that, for me and perhaps for much of my generation, the defining thing about the elderly is simply that: They're old. We see folks with a reduced capacity for movement or hearing or vision and project onto them a reduced capacity for feeling. I thought I knew all about heartbreak when a relationship I had ended after one year. The songs on the radio were written just for me. Nobody writes songs about the broken heart of an eighty-five-year-old. But then and there I started to wonder, "Why don't they?"

I knew I'd be revising my definition of the elderly over the course of this project, but when Grandma decided to join Jason and me on our twelve-thousand-mile journey to interview hundreds of Marriage Masters nationwide, I got to see a side of her I never could have imagined. She had been the original inspiration for the trip, and, overnight, she became the star of the show.

No one could believe that an eighty-eight-year-old woman would traverse the country in an RV with two yahoo bachelors. In fact, she had more energy than Jason and I combined!

When we stumbled groggily out of bed each morning, Grandma was already dressed, purse in hand, ready to launch into a brand-new day. Her wide-armed, wholehearted hugs felt like liquid sunshine. Her exuberance was contagious. Even at the crack of dawn her smile radiated excitement.

While Jason and I ran around like proverbial headless chickens, stressing over a gazillion details and loose ends, Grandma sought the most from each moment.

Grandma refused to nap in the RV. No matter if we had a grueling all-day drive ahead of us, she embraced the scenery like it was an Oscar-winning documentary, refusing to miss a single second. I remember waking up from a little snooze of my own to see her contentedly soaking up the Wyoming plains and roaming buffalo.

Grandma's presence added another dimension to our interviews. Sometimes we visited couples who became tongue-tied and ill at ease in front of the video cameras. But Grandma instantly put them at ease, and brought out the movie star in even the shiest of interviewees.

In Grandma, the couples also found a trustworthy, caring confidante. In Dallas, one woman confided to Grandma she was worried her husband might die soon. How had Grandma coped? she wanted to know.

The scenario repeated itself in New Mexico, Colorado, half a dozen places we visited.

"Nothing can prepare you for losing your spouse," Grandma

told us one night, as we drove through a battering storm along the Oregon coast. "But I do know this. I do know—"

She paused.

"Wait a minute. I'll show you. Pull over and let's get out."

We looked at her like she was crazy. Sheets of rain and gusts of wind slammed into the RV. White, foamy water churned like a washing machine. Rising mist made it impossible to tell where the sky stopped and the ocean began. You couldn't have paid me to get out of that warm RV . . .

. . . But nobody says no to Grandma.

"I've always wanted to stand on the beach in a storm," she said, "and if not now, when?"

She held my arm as we shuffled toward the edge of the sandy embankment. Waves collided and boiled two hundred feet in front of us. The wind was blowing sideways, carrying bits of sand that stung my neck and face. I hunched over, shivering.

"We made it. Fine. Now let's get outta here," I thought, trying to steer Grandma back to the toasty, warm RV.

She shrugged off my grasp.

"Feel this!" she exclaimed, opening her arms wide. "Isn't it wonderful? This is what I wanted you to see."

Rain soaked her hair and clothes, but Grandma had never looked more radiant. As a kid, I felt boundless wonder for moments that grown-ups seemed to miss. Somewhere along the way, however, I lost that wonder. Grandma, apparently, had not.

We listened in silence to the pounding waves. Then she turned to me, an enormous smile on her face.

"Do you know what today is?" she asked.

I shook my head, and her smile grew even wider.

"It's a year later," she told me. "A year from the day we sat in that restaurant, and your mom asked us where we wanted to be."

"No way," I said, my smile matching hers.

"And you know what? I finally have an answer: right here. Doing this, meeting people, traveling with you—well, there's nowhere in the world I'd rather be."

I wrapped my arms around her, no longer feeling the rain or the cold as we hugged.

After a minute, she pulled away, gazing out over the endless ocean serenely.

"When I lost Jack, I lost my whole world," she said, in a soft voice barely distinguishable above the howling wind. "I couldn't see anything except for a gaping hole in my life. I still miss him. It's hard being alone."

She squeezed my hand and turned her gaze from the water to look me in the eyes.

"But I'm still alive," she told me, her smile returning. "And if I'm going to live, I will live fully."

As we journeyed across the nation, couples in their eighties and nineties would drive two, three, four hours to share their stories with us. They struggled to lift their stiff bodies from the car. And they beamed with pride as they sat hand in hand ready to share their gift. I felt humbled by their effort.

One couple in their early nineties—married seventy years!—drove over 250 miles just to meet with us. The husband wore neatly pressed blue slacks, a tan sports coat, and a tie. His wife wore a blue print dress that showed off her blue eyes. As the interview concluded, I asked them, "What is your message for the younger generations?"

They both thought for a second.

Then the husband leaned in, looked me dead in the eye, and with a firm voice said, "I've worked two jobs my whole life, never had a fancy car or a big home. But I have an amazing family and a wife who loves me . . . in my mind, that makes me a wealthy man."

His simple words packed the weight of seventy years' experience. I felt I'd been handed a perspective he'd spent a lifetime attaining.

Two weeks later, we received an email from his granddaughter thanking us for doing the interview. A few days after the interview, she told us, her grandfather had passed away.

Many of the couples we interviewed didn't live to see the completion of this project. We put out the call for their wisdom, and they responded, often going to great lengths to share their stories with us.

We concluded each interview by asking: What was your message for us? After a lifetime of living and loving, what one message would you like to share with the world?

The morning after we had stood together on the beach in the storm, my grandmother and I ate breakfast together in a little diner overlooking the now-calm ocean. I watched her stir cream into her coffee and spread thick raspberry jam over toast, and couldn't keep the smile off my face. She looked different to me now—still radiant, but with a new peacefulness surrounding her like an aura.

Grandma caught me looking and grinned.

"I've finally let go of the anger," she confessed, when I pressed her for an explanation. "Ever since Jack died, I'd been so angry. Not at him," she hastened to add, "but at myself, for not taking advantage of every chance I had to be with him, to appreciate what we had together."

She stirred her coffee and gave a rueful little shrug.

"There was one time at the nursing home, a month before he passed. He asked me to lay down in bed with him—"

"Grandma!" I interrupted, pretending to be shocked, and she laughed and playfully swatted at my arm with her napkin.

"Not like that! Just to take a nap!" she scolded, then grew quiet. For a moment the only sound was her spoon clanking against the side of the coffee cup. "I wouldn't do it," she finally said. "I was worried about what the other residents might think."

She abruptly put the spoon down with a bang. "Who cares what they would have thought! It would have been one more chance to hold him."

I reached out and took her hand, her fingers papery soft but strong as she gave my hand a squeeze in return.

"You always ask couples their message for the younger generation. Here's mine: Make the most of the small moments."

She leaned back in her chair and stretched, gazing out the diner window at the bright, sunshiny day that awaited us. A tiny smile of acceptance, of peace, danced around her lips as she sipped her coffee.

"There's no such thing as a perfect marriage, just perfect moments. Those moments, stacked side by side, fill your life. God gives us a limited number of days. Don't take them for granted, because boy does life go by fast."

That same advice could have been given by any of the couples in this chapter. What follows is their message—their treasure— for all of us.

Goodnight, Sweetheart

Joe and Millie Rozich
Married 65 years

From the outside, the Greystone Ballroom on Woodward Avenue in Detroit may not have looked like much. Squeezed between a rowdy Italian restaurant and the boxing gym where Muhammad Ali would one day get his start, the nondescript building with its soot-darkened walls seemed like nothing special.

But if you pushed through the heavy double doors and ventured inside, you'd find yourself in a place where champagne flowed like water and magic sparkled in the air like the low sweet notes of a blues trumpet. All the biggest bands played at the Greystone when they came to town. Glenn Miller. Artie Lang. Jimmy Campbell. Every Saturday night, they swung and wailed, filling the room with music, with energy, with life. And every

Saturday night, sixteen-year-old Millie put on her best dress and paid a buck-fifty to push through those double doors and dance the night away.

Millie's knockout smile and up-for-anything attitude made every boy in the place want to dance with her. One after another, they'd grab her hand and lead her onto the polished wood floor to dance the fox-trot, the polka, the jitterbug. She'd laugh and twirl and have a terrific time with all of them. But when the band launched into its traditional final song, "Goodnight Sweetheart," any boy hoping for another trip around the dance floor with her was in for a disappointment. Millie always saved the last dance for Joe.

Joe was a quiet, studious boy who didn't care much for dancing. But he *did* care for Millie. *A lot*. So he spent his Saturday nights sitting up in the balcony of the Greystone, listening to the music and watching Millie and the other kids having fun. But as the evening drew to a close, when the lights dimmed and the sax throbbed the first slow, maudlin notes of the final song, Joe headed downstairs and let Millie coax him reluctantly onto the dance floor.

Once he was holding her in his arms, however, he could never remember why he had hesitated.

Six-foot-tall Joe towered over the diminutive Millie, but their bodies seemed to fit perfectly as they waltzed across the dance floor. The huge mirrored ball in the center of the ceiling spangled, casting glittering gems of light and color on the dancers, making the room seem like something out of a fairy tale. And Joe closed his eyes and held Millie a little bit closer, wanting never to let her go.

While a fairy tale setting is the perfect place for a girl who was born on Valentine's Day to meet the man of her dreams and fall in love, Millie and Joe didn't start out having a storybook romance. In fact, Millie barely noticed Joe, even though she saw him practically every day. Joe worked in his father's butcher shop, right next door to the house Millie grew up in. From the first minute he laid eyes on her, Joe knew that she was the one for him. But Millie was too busy having fun to spare much thought for the handsome but serious boy next door.

Joe enlisted the help of Millie's older brother Jimmy to get her to agree to go on a date with him. At first Millie still wasn't interested. Joe seemed nice but dull, like he was moving in slow motion while she was always going a hundred miles an hour. But Jimmy convinced her to give Joe a chance. So one evening, she finally agreed to go see a movie with him.

They got to the theater and settled down in their seats, then Joe reached across and took Millie's hand. Joe's hand was warm and strong, and holding it, Millie felt a first spark of chemistry. Joe didn't let go of her hand for the entire movie, and by the time the credits rolled and the lights came up, the spark had grown into a very real attraction between them. Joe was really something special, she realized. But as much as she was starting to like him, Millie wasn't ready to settle down with anyone just yet. She was seventeen, the music was jumping, the party was happening, and Millie wanted to be in the center of it all.

Joe started showing up at the Greystone Ballroom every Saturday night so he could see Millie. Even though he didn't like to dance, he always let her persuade him to join her for the final waltz. Two years and 110 dances later, Millie let Joe kiss her for the very first time. His patience paid off.

The instant their lips touched, the lightning bolt hit Millie. "Why did I wait so long?" she wondered, wrapping her arms around him and kissing him again. Just like that, Millie fell in love.

To Millie, Joe was like the Greystone Ballroom itself—deceptively unassuming on the outside but full of light and excitement within.

Having waited two years to kiss him, Millie didn't want to wait any longer. A year later they were married, and Millie and Joe finally had their storybook romance together. But even though she had given up the single life, Millie wasn't about to give up dancing.

"C'mon, Joe, let's go! Let's dance!" she'd beg him.

"You do the dancing for us," he'd tease in return, but he always gave in, because he knew how happy it made her.

Millie jumped at any opportunity to dance with her husband. The couple even continued to spend every Saturday night at the Greystone Ballroom, right up until it closed its double doors for good in 1957.

But real life doesn't always have the happy ending that fairy tales do. In 1997, forty years after they danced at the Greystone for the last time, Millie and Joe's own "happily ever after" came to a screeching halt when Joe was diagnosed with Alzheimer's disease.

The couple moved into a senior citizen residence, and Millie spent the next five years caring for Joe as the disease slowly claimed his body and his mind. A series of small strokes impaired Joe's ability to communicate, and his dementia worsened until Millie was finally unable to care for him on her own.

Joe was moved to a hospice, where Millie spent her days sitting at his bedside. Joe no longer recognized Millie or knew her name, but even in the final stages of his illness he still seemed to sense the connection between them. He smiled when she walked into his room in the morning and reached for her hand the second she sat down. He would hold her hand the entire time she was there, just as he had done on their first date, sixty-eight years earlier.

"He was always hanging onto me," Millie remembers, her smile blurred by tears. "He wouldn't let me go."

After nine months at the hospice, Joe couldn't hold on any longer and passed away. He was ninety years old. Millie and Joe had been married for sixty-five years.

A few days before Joe was admitted to the hospice, a three-piece band visited the retirement home where Millie and Joe lived. They played a set of big band songs to entertain the residents and even laid out a temporary dance floor for them.

But for the first time in her life, Millie didn't feel like dancing. Caring for Joe left her exhausted, and the weight of the decision to move him to the hospice had taken its toll. She was sad and scared, and not even the jazzy upbeat tunes she'd loved all her life could lift her spirits.

But as they stood on the sidelines, watching the other seniors dance, a change came over Joe. His shoulders straightened, and his face grew interested and alert. His dementia had progressed to the point where he couldn't recall events that had happened moments earlier, but the music seemed to unlock something in Joe, a part of his mind that remembered all those Saturday nights spent dancing.

Millie smiled and held out her arms, and she and Joe joined the group on the dance floor. Joe's once-strong body was now withered, and his step, which used to be so confident, was halting. Still, he gamely led his wife around the floor.

As they danced, Millie struggled to put her worry aside and enjoy herself. But when the music ended and the band bade the crowd good night, she was relieved. She made her way to a chair and wearily sank down. But Joe didn't join her.

He stood in front of her, with an expectant expression she didn't at first understand.

But when he grimaced and gestured at the now-empty dance floor, she realized what he wanted.

"They've finished playing. Have a seat," she said.

But he gestured to the dance floor again, agitated.

"Sit down, Joe," Millie repeated.

Joe shook his head. He tried to find the words locked away in his mind. He grabbed Millie's hand, tugging at it, trying to make her get up and dance.

After the countless times she had urged Joe to dance with her, this was the first time he had ever been the one trying to persuade her.

The irony and tragedy of it overwhelmed her, and Millie's eyes filled with tears.

"No, Joe, it's over," she said, feeling something inside her crumble as she realized the deep truth to her words. "The music's stopped, there's no more dancing, we're done."

But Joe was insistent. He squeezed her hand and looked urgently at her.

"Last dance!" he said.

Millie's eyes widened. In recent months, the Alzheimer's had robbed Joe of the ability to form sentences or articulate coherent thoughts, and when he did speak, it was in a slurred mumble. But those two words came out crystal clear.

"Last dance."

And then, just as if he had snapped his fingers and commanded it, the band started to play again, one final song for the crowd, a good-night waltz.

It was miraculous.

It was magic.

Joe smiled at Millie, proud and satisfied. "Last dance!"

So for both the first and last time, Millie let Joe coax her reluctantly onto the empty dance floor.

As Joe pulled her into the familiar *one*-two-three, *one*-two-three, his arms strengthened around her and his step grew more steady. This was *their* dance, after all.

Millie looked into the ravaged face of this man broken by illness, mere days away from entering hospice care, and saw Joe. *Her* Joe, the Joe she had married. For the first time in months, maybe in years, Joe was present, he was himself, he *remembered*.

Millie was sure of it—she could see it in his face as they began to waltz.

The audience saw it too. A cheer rose as the seniors, many of whom knew Joe and Millie, and knew the trial they were undergoing, got to their feet, applauding. No one else joined the couple, content just to watch Millie and Joe gliding around the floor. They knew that this was Joe and Millie's last song, last hurrah, last dance.

"Look at 'em go!" one lady cried out, moved, both tears and laughter in her voice. "Joe's still dancing!"

The crowd cheered again, then gradually fell silent. Their faces filled with longing, for their own past dances, lost loves, forgotten grace. Watching Millie and Joe, they were transported back to their own dancing days, at the Savoy Ballroom in New York, the Regency in Los Angeles, the Trocadero in Denver.

But for Millie it was the Greystone Ballroom in Detroit, always and forever. The garishly decorated walls of the senior center fell away, and for one last dance, she was back at her old stomping ground on Woodward Avenue and Joe was holding her close. He was young again, and healthy, and Millie was seventeen, with a future ahead of her filled with so much dizzying joy and possibility that she needed Joe's strong arms to hold her steady.

Too soon, too soon, the song came to an end. The music stopped, the lights came up, and Millie and Joe had to move apart. Their last dance was over.

But while the song lasted only a few moments, Millie and Joe had been dancing for sixty-five years. And in Millie's dreams and memories and heart, somewhere music is playing and they're still dancing. . . .

"Time flies!" she says. "There are a lot of things I never got to do with Joe.

"My advice is to never pass on an opportunity to create a moment with your mate. Each moment is more precious than you might think."

We May Not Have Much, But . . .

Russell and Betsey Byrd
Married 51 years

"Fifty years," Betsey mused, carefully putting the last plate into the dishwasher and closing the door. She started the machine, then carried her cup of chicory coffee over to the kitchen table and sank onto one of the sturdy maple chairs. "Can you believe it's been fifty years?"

"Fifty wonderful years," Russell answered.

He set down the beignet he was eating and reached into his pocket, pulling out a tiny blue box. He set it down in front of her, next to the box of pastries from Morning Call, the New Orleans coffee shop where Russell had picked up their breakfast.

Betsey's jaw dropped when she saw the box. "What did you do?!" she asked happily, picking it up delicately, as though if she seemed too eager, it would disappear.

"Seems to me if we're going to get married again, we ought to do it right this time," Russell answered, unable to hide a proud smile.

Betsey opened the box and let out a gasp. Nestled inside on a velvet cushion were two gold wedding bands. They were the most beautiful things Betsey had ever seen.

She jumped up and threw her arms around her husband, who hugged her back, laughing.

"Do you like them?"

"I love them!" Betsey said, sitting back down and admiring the rings some more. They seemed to capture the sunlight streaming in through the grand French windows, their dazzling reflection brightening the comfortable, elegant room. Betsey stroked one of the rings with the tip of her finger, then held up her hand, regarding the plain metal band already adorning her fourth finger.

"Of course, I love the ring you gave me fifty years ago," she told her husband, "but . . ."

Betsey trailed off. She truly did love the wedding band she was already wearing. Although it was plain and cheap, it was the only ring Russell had been able to afford at the time, and all that had mattered to her was the love with which it was offered. That was still all that mattered, really . . . although the sight of the new rings took her breath away.

". . . But you deserve something as pretty as you are," Russell finished for her, and Betsey had to get up from her chair and hug him again.

For months now, the focus of Betsey and Russell's days was planning the ceremony the couple was going to have when they renewed their wedding vows. This time, they vowed, they were going to do it right.

In 1955, when they had gotten married for the first time, they hadn't been able to afford to throw the kind of celebration they wanted. They were both in their twenties and worked hard just to put food on the table and make the rent on their no-frills one-bedroom apartment. They barely had enough money for the basic necessities, and anything left over at the end of the month went straight into the bank, where they were saving up for the down payment on a house.

All those years of pinching pennies and clipping coupons finally paid off. The couple had saved enough money to buy their dream home, a large, comfortable house in a quiet New Orleans neighborhood where they could settle down and raise their kids.

Betsey looked around at her beautiful, luxurious home and gave a contented sigh. They had been living there for more than thirty years, and in that time, Betsey had filled the house with items she loved. Everywhere she looked she saw a treasure, a memory of the wonderful years she and Russell had spent together.

The clay pencil holder their oldest daughter had made in kindergarten, which still occupied a prominent place on the counter under the phone, even though their daughter lived a couple of hours away and had a kindergartner of her own now. The dark blue rug, which they were so eager to bring home that they couldn't wait the six weeks it would have taken to have it delivered, so they tied it precariously to the top of the car and drove it home themselves, creeping along at ten miles an hour the entire way, since they were so worried about it falling off. Even the chairs they were sitting in now painted a vivid, specific picture in Betsey's mind: As much as she had admired their graceful, sweeping lines and glossy polished wood, she'd cried when Russell brought them home, because it meant replacing the chairs they had brought with them from their first apartment, cheap pressboard ones that were falling apart but brought back memories of their own.

Even when the couple had nothing, when they were at the very beginning of their marriage and struggling just to survive, they would light candles and sit in those chairs, their dinner growing cold as they talked a mile a minute about their plans and dreams for the future.

And now the future was here. Their golden anniversary was coming up, and they were going to celebrate in style.

But their plans were about to take an unexpected turn.

It was hurricane season in New Orleans, and the evening news reported a big storm forming over the Bahamas and crossing into Florida.

"Another storm," Russell said as he clicked off the TV.

But it wasn't just another storm. It was a hurricane the weather people named Katrina, and the next morning, August 24, 2005, it landed in Florida.

The order came to evacuate New Orleans, but Russell and Betsey weren't overly alarmed. Part of living on the Gulf Coast was dealing with the weather. They'd been forced to evacuate the house several times before, for other tropical storms, and had always been able to return the next day with no damage worse than the occasional broken tree branch. So they were sure that this time it would be the same.

Betsey grabbed the box with their tax documents, baptismal certificates, and house title, and carried it out to the car. Russell locked the door securely behind them. They left the pictures on the wall and the photo albums on the bookshelf.

The couple drove off to a relative's house in Opelousas,

Louisiana, to wait out the storm, leaving behind a houseful of memories, a lifetime of love. They had no idea that they would never be able to live there again, that they were saying good-bye to a lifetime's worth of possessions.

Two hours later, they arrived at Betsey's sister's house in Opelousas. Mary and Eugene Casey welcomed them with relief.

"It's a bad one," Eugene said, flipping through the channels on the TV, report after report of the destruction Katrina was starting to wreak. "It might be the worst storm yet."

The couple spent the next few days glued to the TV, barely able to believe the images they were seeing of their beloved city. Gone were any thoughts of their anniversary or planning the party. Katrina became the only thing that existed in the world.

Numbly, they watched the exodus from the flooding Gulf Coast. Just when they thought the worst was over, the levees— the 17th Street Canal, the London Avenue Canal, the Industrial Canal—broke, and the city was under water.

Russell and Betsey gripped each other's hands as the television broadcast stories of the deaths, the damage.

"It's gone," Russell whispered. Their city, their house, their normal life—everything had been washed away in the storm. "Everything's gone."

Their neighborhood was submerged in eight feet of water. In their home, the canal water reached nearly to the ceiling, destroying everything it touched.

Diplomas, discharge notices, baby photos. Pictures from their wedding in 1955, pictures from their five children's marriages. Christmas ornaments, clothing, the kitchen chairs with their curved maple legs, and the beautiful golden rings for their marriage renewal ceremony—everything Russell and Betsey owned that symbolized their years together had been ruined in the flood.

They had insurance to cover the cost of the house and their possessions, but the things they lost were priceless, irreplaceable. There were so many things that no amount of money could ever buy back.

Their dreams of a lavish wedding ceremony had also been washed away by Katrina. When the weekend of their fiftieth anniversary arrived, Russell and Betsey couldn't handle a big celebration with lots of guests. They hardly felt like celebrating at all; they just wanted to be by themselves.

So they got in their car and drove to the Holiday Inn in Opelousas. They checked into a room and ordered dinner from room service. When it arrived, Betsey lit candles, Russell dimmed the lights, and they sat down together.

As Betsey gazed at her husband of fifty years over the small hotel table, she shook her head, as much in wonder as regret.

She could barely believe how far they'd come from their first tiny apartment, when they'd had absolutely nothing in the world but each other.

And now they once again found themselves alone, without money or possessions.

But just like that first time, Betsey realized, they could get through this, they could survive. Even though they had lost their possessions, they still had their memories. They still had each other.

As the Byrds walk through their gutted New Orleans home, Russell steps through the frames of what used to be an interior wall of their living room. "We've had a good life together," he says.

Betsey sighs, looking at the wall where all of their family photos had once hung. Eight feet up, a line of moldy residue marks how high the stagnant, filthy water had risen. "We lost so many things," she says. "But we still have our family and we still have each other."

As they come together in the dining room, they put their arms around each other. "It's times like this when you realize what's important in life," Russell says.

Betsey nods and clings tighter to her husband. "We still have our love."

Adventures with Grandpa Buck—by Jason

Russell Mohn
Married 64 years

Deep into a particularly tedious stretch of Marriage Master interview marathons in Northern California, our ninth straight day at senior retirement centers, Mat and I were feeling mentally deep fried. The process doesn't seem all that difficult on paper, I know, because, really, how much effort can it take to sit on a couch, eat cookies, and listen to love stories all day long? But after back-to-back, to-back, to-back, to-back, to-back, to-back, to-back hour-long Q&A sessions (notice how tiresome it is just *reading* back-to-back seven times in a row), we were reduced to mumbling, stumbling fools with narratives about love and marriage and grandkids named Carlyle, Samantha, and Chuck (who lives in Topeka) swirling and mixing in the mushy space between our ears. Mat likened the information overload to trying to take a drink from a fire hose. I was starting to slip into daydreams about delicious lime-green Jell-O desserts.

The retirement center had huge skylights on the ceiling, constantly reminding me how hot and gorgeous it was outside. I stared longingly at the blue sky portals as we shuffled slowly among a throng of seniors in the midday pilgrimage to the dining hall. "This is no place for a twenty-eight-year-old," I secretly pouted. "Not on a day like this."

Midway through my delicious lime-green Jell-O dessert, a retirement center specialty, a sporty looking eighty-nine-year-old by the name of Russell Mohn leaned in from a nearby table. "My first wife passed away after thirty-six years of marriage and I've been with my second wife for twenty-eight. Do I make the cut?"

"Sure," Mat said, "but we have only one time slot open, right after lunch."

"Oh, well that won't do," he said, shifting his thick-rimmed eyeglasses higher on his nose. "That's when I go down to my swimmin' hole."

¿Qué? My eyes lit up. "Sir, did you just say *swimmin' hole*?"

Ten minutes later, we were speeding through twisty, back-country roads in Russell's brand-spanking-new Mini Cooper.

"This rides pretty nice, Russell," I said from the back seat.

"Oh, you haven't seen nothin' yet," he said with a grin, his hand reaching for the gearshift. "Listen to this engine spin!"

Vrrooooom! He downshifted quickly, lurching the little machine forcefully through a curve. Russell chuckled, delighted; we grabbed our Jesus handles, nervous.

After winding up and around and down a rather narrow, gravel mountain road (testing the engine's performance capabilities all the way), we arrived at a forest trailhead. Mat and I looked at each other, wide-eyed, while Russell grabbed a long coil of rope from his trunk and hefted it over his shoulder.

"What's that for, Russ?" Mat asked.

"We have a little climb ahead of us," he replied.

Mat and I shot each other another look: *Is this guy for real?*

After a half-mile trek into the forest, we stood at the top of a steep, one-hundred-foot embankment, peering down into a river ravine. Russell set to work with his rope, somehow configuring carabiners and rope loops and secret Eagle Scout knots around trees into a makeshift climbing harness. Eighty-nine years old. *This guy is for real.*

"Russ, isn't that poison oak there?" I asked, pointing to the devil plant responsible for so many hellish nights of itchy, oozing rashes in my youth, a big patch of which he'd been standing in for ten minutes.

"Yep," he said, "doesn't much bother me."

Of course not . . . and why would it? I shuddered.

Russell tested his harness with a tug on the rope, then started to scale backward down the embankment. I'm not saying it was a ninety-degree drop-off, or even a cliff, because Mat and I were able to get down to the bottom of this thing without the rope, but it was steep—vertical enough to force us to hold on to trees and branches the whole way down (even so, we slipped and slid on our butts a couple of times). And we were twenty-eight years old!

While we stumbled down to the river beside the rappelling Russell, we talked about the fifty-plus mountaineering adventures he'd been on with his current wife, Jane. Their treks took them up the Cascade Mountains, the Sierras, and deep into Havasu Canyon, "the Shangri-la of America." "My first wife was all right at mountaineering and spelunking," he said, "but she liked to use pack mules too much for my taste. Now Jane's a real champion on the trails."

"Does she ever join you down here?" Mat asked.

"She used to, sure," he replied, "but she got a bad hip at seventy-five and had to stop."

The river we found at the bottom of the ravine was absolutely beautiful: pristine, cool-but-not-cold water, crystal-clear visibility to the bottom, and just deep enough to jump into from the surrounding boulders. I set up the video camera for the interview while Mat stripped off his shirt and shoes and jumped from the rocks with a cannonball splash. In the meantime, Russell came out from behind a boulder and made a big splash of his own.

"Hope you guys don't mind," he called out without an ounce of self-consciousness, "but I only swim in the nude."

I'll never forget the look on Mat's face as he emerged out of the water onto the boulder where Russell was perched, buck naked, blowing up a hot pink floaty mattress: *What the—?*

We didn't spend much of the hour asking questions about marriage that day down at the river. Mostly, the three of us just kicked back on a boulder in the middle of the river (two of us partially clothed, the other not), soaking up the sun and talking about Russell's mountaintop rescues, broken bones, and other daring adventures. But there was one question we didn't forget: "Russell, if you could leave us with one message, what would it be?"

He looked down at his reflection in the water, pondering his response. Then, as if telling us a rueful secret, he answered in a quiet tone. "The hardest thing about living in a retirement home is watching the people who've decided to stop living. It's a subtle thing. I don't even know if you can tell by looking at them.

But it's there. It's as if they've reached a certain age and decided to *be* elderly.

"I've climbed more mountains than I can remember. I've had two memorable, fulfilling marriages. And whether it's a mountain peak or a beautiful relationship, the one thing I've learned is that life is all about attitude. Someone once told me that his marriage had grown stale. I don't buy that. Marriages don't get stale—*people* get stale.

"Love, life, age—it's all a state of mind. You want an everlasting marriage, right? That's why you're here? Well, my advice to the young people out there is this: It's absolutely, one hundred percent possible . . . but only if you believe it's possible."

With that, he grabbed his pink floaty and trumpeted: "Fellas, I'd love to stay down here longer, but it's Saturday, and Jane and I never miss *The Lawrence Welk Show.* Now let's get back up that hill!"

Ten-four, Grandpa Buck. Your message has been received.

The Bachelorword

THIS IS WHAT I NEEDED TO HEAR

—by Jason

After enlisting in Project Everlasting, I felt a sharp shift in my "purpose" for being involved in the mission. Over time, I found myself taking great interest in our interviewees' answers. I watched closely for their nonverbal communication techniques and probed deeper into their stories. I asked the husbands what they did to make their wives feel cared for. I took scrupulous notes when the wives described the aspects they appreciated most about their husbands and what they could do without. No longer was I on board purely for buddy-buddy road trips and chicky-poo pickup lines. I began genuinely to care about marriage.

Midway through the tour, we found ourselves in the Oak Park neighborhood of Chicago, setting up for an interview with Marriage Masters Keith and Vicki Cady.

"You'll make your wife very happy someday, Jason," Keith told me. "You're going to be a great husband."

Not knowing what else to say, I smiled respectfully and said, "Thank you, sir." Inside, I questioned how he could be so sure.

I'd heard the same statement before from grandmas who were convinced that I'd make perfect marriage material (I *am* tall, after all). But the way the ninety-one-year-old man said it made me take special notice. The way he spoke hinted he was a kindred spirit, someone who had once been in my same shoes, or maybe it was the look on his face: so sincere, sure-footed and wise, as if he'd found a vantage point from which to see things with more clarity than anybody else, even me. He seemed to be looking right into my heart.

Maybe he was able to see something I couldn't see?

Which brings me to my personal discovery, the biggest lesson that I've taken from my four years on this mission called Project Everlasting: Marriage Masters made mistakes. They still make mistakes—and plenty! In fact, looking back across the two hundred–plus couples we went to for marital wisdom, I can't remember one relationship that didn't have a time line dotted with a few failures, some minor and some monumental. But, see, I've discovered that this is the beauty of these couples' stories. They were brave enough and determined enough to work through those failures and, for the most part, fix them. The true beauty of lifelong marriage isn't expressed in the measure of gushy-gushy affection these senior citizens were able emit for us on the couch, but rather in the history of their courage. As they showed time and time again, lifelong love is not for the faint of heart. From the moment a Marriage Master like Keith Cady made his vow to his young bride, Vicki—not knowing who she was going to become or how she would change over the years, not knowing who *he* would become or how *he* would change over the years, not knowing what emotional strife and ugliness would come between them some days, not knowing how many times he would have to suck up his pride and ask for forgiveness, not knowing that some of her most adorable peccadilloes might eventually become the most irritating nuisances and not fully understanding just *how* bad "worse" could get nor *how* unconditionally loving he'd need to be in order to honor and respect her, yet trusting in himself, that he'd somehow, some way live up to his vows and, still more impressively, trusting that his bride would do everything in her power to do the same for him—to now, sixty-nine years later, admitting that he's fallen short in many ways but is still man enough to try harder and recommit to doing better every day. . . .

Sweet goodness, now *that's* the courage I want!

And I'm getting there, thanks to the hundreds of strangers, some of whom aren't with us anymore, God rest their souls, who chose to open up their lives to Mat and me . . . and you. I've discovered that a great husband is a brave husband and a great marriage is the result of countless acts of undaunted love. Hence, my new motto: Let no relationship of mine suffer from my lack of courage.

Finally, to Keith Cady and the scores of grandmas who saw something in me, I hope you'll all still be around to see my progress one day, because I'm going to make my wife very happy.

I'm going to be a *great* husband.

WAX ON, WAX OFF

—by Mat

I set out on this crazy book endeavor with the intention of discovering mind-stretching, concept-busting, esoteric truths about the world of everlasting love. I wanted deep, undiscovered secrets. I desired a brand-new formula that, when practiced concisely, leads to a rock-solid, indestructible marriage, a marriage with a foundation so strong that no crisis or tragedy could rip it apart. Elusive, magical words that had never before been uttered.

For the sake of the story, Jason and I figured it would be useful to get some man-on-the-street interviews to contrast with the Marriage Masters' thought-provoking wisdom. So, one night, midway through our trip, we walked into a quintessential dive bar in downtown Detroit, where flickering neon beer signs lit up the windows. Other than Bob, a fifty-year-old thrice-married drunken bar hound who had his arm wrapped around Kitty, a twenty-something never-married college dropout, the bar was empty. "Ahh, the perfect counterpart to our wise elders," I thought.

"So what do you think the secrets are to a successful marriage?" I asked. Jason zoomed the video camera in tight on their faces in order to catch every slurred, naïve response.

Kitty leaned on Bob's shoulder, eager to answer the question. "We-e-l-l-l, you need to have commitment," she started, "you can't give up. Marriage is something you have to work at. Oh, and you gotta communicate. It takes a lot of communication."

Jason looked out from behind the camera and gave me his *not bad* face.

Then Bob jumped in. "Let me tell you something about marriage. You can't try to change the person. You have to accept the other person and respect her. Yeah, respect, that's probably the most important thing in a marriage."

"And love!" Kitty exclaimed, giving Bob a big kiss on the cheek.

"Yeah, you just love me because I buy you beer," replied Bob.

"Did someone say beer?" Kitty asked. "We need another round." She pulled Bob by the shirt back to the bar and ordered two more Coronas.

Wait a minute. *They* weren't supposed to know the secrets to marriage!

Obviously, what I'd been learning from our Marriage Masters wasn't all that revelatory. Still, I couldn't escape the bigger question: If Mr. Thrice Divorced knew what it took to succeed at marriage, why hadn't he? If the secrets to matrimonial bliss are that obvious, why is our divorce rate so high? What's missing?

Throughout our Project Everlasting adventure, I've felt like Daniel LaRusso in the movie *The Karate Kid*. Daniel sought out Mr. Miyagi because he wanted to learn karate. For weeks Mr. Miyagi put him to work sanding floors, painting fences, and waxing cars. Frustrated that he hadn't learned a single karate move, Daniel decided to quit. As he was leaving, Mr. Miyagi called him to the freshly sanded deck and asked Daniel to demonstrate his "paint the fence" motion. As he did so, Mr. Miyagi threw a punch and Daniel blocked it perfectly. "Sand the floor" became a kick block. "Waxing cars" became, well, some other kind of important block, but you get the point. Daniel realized he had been learning karate all along.

After that bar meeting, I sat with couples feeling like Daniel obliviously painting the fence. I felt discouraged. I was ready to quit. I hadn't learned anything my generation didn't already know.

But somewhere in the midst of all the interviews, I began recognizing the wisdom in the Marriage Masters' words. It was as if every interview was a small step up the side of a mountain. Each step in itself felt small and insignificant, but I ultimately climbed high enough to realize that these couples had provided me with a whole new perspective on marriage, and I know their gifts will probably continue to unfold for me as I grow and find my own love story.

In the end, the greatest gift I've received on this incredible journey is hope. Hope that one day I too could be sitting hand-in-hand with my wife, celebrating fifty years of love. Time and time again I've sat with couples whose connection seemed so tangible I could almost see it. They are proof that lifelong love is possible. The Marriage Masters have also demonstrated to me that it's possible to overcome the most daunting of marital mountains, to traverse the bleakest of valleys, and still return to love. One day when I'm facing my own perilous landscapes, I will think back to these couples who have become living testaments to my childhood belief and remember that love really can conquer all.

So my friends, wax on, wax off. I know I plan to, until Miyagi shows up and offers that path to me. And one day, with any luck, I'll be able to look over at my wife on our fiftieth wedding anniversary and think back to these couples who paved the way and say, "Thank you."

Acknowledgments

With a project of this scope and magnitude, we know well that we couldn't have pulled it off without an incredible support system of loving, generous, and immensely talented team members. The following people have been Project Everlasting angels, integral pieces for bringing this dream to fruition.

We have to start out by thanking each couple who opened their homes and hearts to us in an effort to support those who desire lifelong love stories.

To our amazing families—thank you!

Mat: To my parents, Mary and Haven, thank you for your constant encouragement and living example of mature love. To my brothers, John, Rich, Michael, Matthew, and my sis, Jennifer, and their families, thank you for your belief in me.

Jason: To my Marriage Master grandparents, Hank and Anne Leenknecht and Russell and Letha Miller; to my lil' bros and sisters, Greg, Kevin, Anna, and Cara; and to my ultimate role models for loving marriage, Mary Jo and Merlin—you can't be thanked enough.

To the Project Everlasting team: Christopher Lutz, Pamela Potts, Jessica Schulte, Chris Lacambra, Christian Anderson, Deb Gee, Chad St. Cyr, Heather Westing, Jacquie Barnbrook, Camille

Cellucci, Monica Beck, Leslie Chotiner, Adam Krim, Karina Grotz, Dilara Esengil, and, most of all, Grandma Dorothy—thank you for your relentless efforts in manifesting this dream.

Thank you, Amanda Patten, the sweetest editor two bachelors could ask for. To our beautiful super-agent, Lisa Grubka, for her persuasive prowess. To Christy Scatteralla, thank you for your vision and talent bringing this book to life. Thank you, Aury Wallington, Kuwana Haulsey, Courtenay Hameister, Dan Krow, and Angela Allen, for your skillful wordsmithing. Thank you, Mark Victor Hansen, for teaching us how to dream-build; Marianne Williamson, for your kind words and inspiration; Fleetwood RVs, for the road tour's 36-foot Bachelormobile.

Special thanks to Ken and Helen Kleinberg and Mary Manin Morrissey, for putting your resources and energy behind this project.

Finally, thank you, God, for choosing us to be the bearer of your dream.